Hell

"The Dogma of Hell, Illustrated by Facts Taken from Profane and Sacred History."

By

Francois Xavier Schouppe, S.J.

Edited by
Paul A. Böer, Sr.

VERITATIS SPLENDOR PUBLICATIONS
et cognoscetis veritatem et veritas liberabit vos (Jn 8:32)

MMXIII

Cover Art
FRANCKEN, Frans II
The Last Judgement
1606
Oil on copper, 67 x 52 cm
Private collection

This is a re-publication of a work found in:

Hell: The Dogma of Hell Illustrated by Facts Taken from Profane and Sacred History . F.X. Schouppe, S.J.. (New York: Hickey & Co., 1883).

Retypeset and republished in 2013 by Veritatis Splendor Publications.

AD MAJOREM DEI GLORIAM

CONTENTS

I. THE DOGMA OF HELL

The Dogma of Hell is the most terrible truth of our faith. There *is* a hell. We are sure of it as of the existence of God, the existence of the sun. Nothing, in fact, is more clearly revealed than the dogma of hell, and Jesus Christ proclaims it as many as fifteen times in the Gospel.

Reason comes to the support of revelation; the existence of a hell is in harmony with the immutable notions of justice engraved in the human heart. Revealed to men from the beginning, and conformable to natural reason, this dreadful truth has always been, and is still known, by all nations not plunged by barbarism in complete ignorance.

Hell never has been denied by heretics, Jews or Mohammedan. The pagans themselves have retained their belief in it, although the errors of paganism may have impaired in their minds the sound notion.

It has been reserved for modern and contemporaneous atheism, carried to the pitch of delirium, to outdo the impiety of all ages by denying the existence of hell.

There are, in our day, men who laugh at, question, or openly deny the reality of hell.

They laugh at hell; but the universal belief of nations should not be laughed at; a matter affecting the everlasting destiny of man is not laughable; there is no fun, when the question is of enduring for eternity the punishment of fire.

They question, or even deny the dogma of hell; but on a matter of religious dogma, they cannot decide without being competent; they cannot call in doubt, still less deny, a belief so solidly established, without bringing forward irrefutable reasons.

Now, are they who deny the dogma of hell competent in matters of religion? Are they not strangers to that branch of the sciences, which is called theology? Are they not oftenest ignorant of the very elements of religion, taught in the Catechism?

Whence, then, proceeds the mania, of grappling with a religious question which is not within their province? Why such warmth in combating the belief in hell? Ah! It is interest that prompts them; they are concerned about the non-existence of hell, knowing that if there is a hell, it shall be their portion; these unhappy men wish that there might not be one, and they try to persuade themselves that there is none. In fact, these efforts usually end in a sort of incredulity. At bottom, this disbelief is only a doubt, but a doubt which unbelievers formulate by a negation.

Accordingly, they say there is no hell. And upon what reasons do they rest so bold a denial? All their reasons and arguments may be summed up in the following assertions:

"I do not believe in hell."

"They who affirm this dogma know nothing about it; the future life is an insoluble problem, and invincible, *perhaps*."

"No one has returned from beyond the grave to testify that there is a hell."

These are all the proofs, all the theology of the teachers of impiety. Let us examine.

1. *I do not believe in it.* You do not believe in hell? And there is no hell, because you do not believe in it? Will hell exist any the less, because you do not please to believe in it? Should a thief be so foolish as to deny that there is a prison, would the prison cease to exist, and should the thief not enter it?

2. You say that the future life is a problem, and hell a *perhaps.* You are deceived; this problem is fully solved by revelation, and left in no uncertainty.

But suppose for a moment, that there was an uncertainty, that the existence of eternal torments is only probable, and that it may be said: *perhaps there is no hell;* I ask any man of sound reason, would he not be the silliest of men who, upon such a *perhaps*, should expose himself to the punishment of an everlasting fire?

3. They say that no one returned from beyond the grave o tell us about hell. If it were true that no one has returned, would hell exist the less? Is it the dammed who ought to teach us that there is a hell? It might as well be said that it is prisoners who ought to inform us that there are prisons. To know that there is a hell it is not necessary that the damned should come to tell us; God's word is sufficient for us; God it is who publishes it, and informs the world concerning it.

But are you, who claim that no dead person has returned to speak of hell, quite sure of it? You say it, you declare it; but you have against you historical, proved, unexceptionable facts. I do not speak here of Jesus Christ, who descended into hell, and rose again from the dead; there are other dead persons who returned to life, and damned souls who have revealed their everlasting reprobation. Still, whatever may be the historical certainty of this sort of facts, I repeat, it is not upon this ground that we claim to establish the dogma of hell; that truth is known to us by the infallible word of God; the facts which we adduce serve but to confirm, and place it in a clearer light.

II. MANIFESTATIONS OF HELL

As we have just said, the dogma of hell stands on the infallible word of God; but in his mercy, God, to aid our faith, permits at intervals, the truth of hell to be manifested in a sensible manner. These manifestations are more frequent than is thought; and when supported by sufficient proofs, they are unexceptionable facts, which must be admitted like all the other facts of history.

Here is one of these facts. It was juridically proved in the process of canonization of St. Francis of Jerome, and under oath attested by a large number of eye-witnesses. In the year 1707, St. Francis of Jerome was preaching, as was his wont, in the neighborhood of the city of Naples. He was speaking of hell and the awful chastisements that await obstinate sinners. A brazen courtesan who lived there, troubled by a discourse which aroused her remorse, sought to hinder it by jests and shouts, accompanied by noisy instruments. As she was standing close to the window, the Saint cried out: "*Beware, my daughter, of resisting grace; before eight days God will punish you.*" The unhappy creature grew only more boisterous. Eight days elapsed, and the holy preacher happened to be again before the same house. This time she was silent, the windows were shut. The hearers, with dismay on their faces, told the Saint that Catherine -- that was the name of the bad woman -- had a few hours before died suddenly. *"Died!"* he repeated, *"well, let her tell us now what she has gained by laughing at hell. Let us ask her."* He uttered these words in an inspired tone, and every one expected a miracle. Followed by an immense crowd, he went up to the death chamber, and there, after having prayed for an instant, he uncovers the face of the corpse, and says in a loud voice, *"Catherine, tell us where art thou now."* At this summons, the dead woman lifts her head, while opening her wild eyes, her face borrows color, her features assume an expression of horrible despair, and in a mournful voice, she pronounces these words: *"In hell; I am in hell."* And immediately, she falls back again into the condition of a corpse.

"I was present at that event," says one of the witnesses who deposed before the Apostolic tribunal, "but I never could convey the impression it produced on me and the bystanders, nor that which I still feel every time I pass that house and look at that window. At the sight of that ill-fated abode, I still hear the pitiful cry resounding: *"In hell; I am in hell."* (Father Bach, *Life of St. Francis of Jerome.)*

Ratbod, King of the Frisons, who is mentioned in ecclesiastical history in the eighth century, had said to St. Wolfrand that he was not afraid of hell; that he wished to be there with the kings, his ancestors, and most illustrious personages. *"Moreover,"* he added, *"later on, I shall be always able to receive baptism."* *"Lord,"* answered the Saint, *"do not neglect the grace that is offered to thee. The God who offers the sinner pardon, does not promise him to-morrow."* The King did not heed this advice, and put off his conversion. A year after, learning the arrival of St. Willibrord, he dispatched an officer to him, to invite him to come to the court and confer baptism on him. The Saint answered that it was too late. *"Your master,"* he said, *"died after your departure. He braved eternal fire; he has fallen into it. I have seen him this night, loaded with fiery chains, in the bottom of the abyss."*

Here is another witness from beyond the grave. History avers that when St. Francis Xavier was at Cangoxima, in Japan, he performed a great number of miracles, of which the most celebrated was the resurrection of a maiden of noble birth. This young damsel died in the flower of her age, and her father, who loved her dearly, believed he would become crazy. Being an idolater, he had no resources in his affliction, and his friends, who came to console him, rendered his grief only the more poignant.

Two neophytes, who came to see him before the funeral of her whom he mourned day and night, advised him to seek help from the holy man who was doing such great things, and demand from him with confidence, the life of his daughter. The pagan -- persuaded by the neophytes that nothing was impossible to the European bonze, and beginning to hope against all human appearances, as is usual with the afflicted, who readily believe whatever comforts them -- goes to Father Francis, falls at his feet, and, with tears in his eyes, entreats him to bring to life again his only daughter whom he has just lost, adding that it would be to give life to himself.

Xavier, touched by the faith and sorrow of the pagan, went aside with his companion, Fernando, to pray to God. Having come back again after a short time, *"Go,"* he said to the afflicted father, *"your daughter is alive!"*

The idolater, who expected that the Saint would come with him to his house and invoke the name of the God of the Christians over his daughter's body, took this speech as a jest and withdrew, dissatisfied. But scarcely had he gone a few steps when he saw one of his servants, who, all beside himself with joy, shouted from a distance that his daughter was alive.

Presently, he beheld her approaching. After the first embraces the daughter related to her father that, as soon as she had expired, two horrible demons pounced upon her, and sought to hurl her into a fiery abyss; but that two men, of a venerable and modest appearance, snatched her from the hands of these executioners and restored her life, she being unable to tell how it happened.

The Japanese understood who were these two men of whom his daughter spoke, and he led her directly to Xavier to return him such thanks as so great a favour deserved. She no sooner saw the Saint with his companion, Fernando, than she exclaimed: *"There are my two deliverers!"* and, at the same time, the daughter and the father demanded baptism.

The servant of God, Bernard Colnago, a religious of the Company of Jesus, died at Catana in the odor of sanctity, in the year 1611. We read in his biography that he prepared for the passage by a life full of good works and the constant remembrance of death, so apt to engender a holy life. To keep in mind this salutary remembrance, he preserved in his little cell a skull, which he had placed upon a stand to have it always before his eyes. One day it struck him that, perhaps, that head had been the abode of a mind rebellious to God, and now the object of

His wrath. Accordingly, he begged the Sovereign Judge to enlighten him, and to cause the skull to shake if the spirit that had animated it was burning in hell. No sooner had he finished his prayer than it shook with a horrible trembling, a palpable sign that it was the skull of a damned soul.

This saintly religious, favored with singular gifts, knew the secret of consciences, and, sometimes, the decrees of God's justice. One day God revealed to him the eternal perdition of a young libertine, who was his parents' heart-scald. The unfortunate young man, after having rushed into all sorts of dissipation, was slain by an enemy. His mother, at the sight of so sad an end, conceived the liveliest terrors for her son's everlasting salvation, and besought Father Bernard to tell her in what state his soul was. Despite her entreaties Father Bernard did not answer by a single word, sufficiently showing by his silence that he had nothing consoling to say. He was more explicit to one of her friends. This person inquiring why he did not give an answer to an afflicted mother, the religious openly said to him that he was unwilling to increase her affliction; that this young libertine was damned, and that, during his prayer, God had shown him the youth under a hideous and frightful aspect.

On the 1st of August, 1645, there died in the odor of sanctity, at the College of Evora, in Portugal, Anthony Pereyra, Coadjutor Brother of the Company of Jesus. His history is, perhaps the strangest furnished by the annals of this Society. In 1599, five years after his entrance into the novitiate, he was seized by a mortal malady in the Isle of St. Michael, one of the Azores; and a few moments after he had received the last sacraments, beneath the eyes of the whole community, who were present at his agony, he seemed to expire, and became cold like a corpse. The appearance -- almost imperceptible -- of a slight throbbing of the heart alone, prevented his immediate burial. Accordingly, he was left three whole days on his death-bed, and there were already plain signs of decomposition in the body, when all of a sudden, on the fourth day, he opened his eyes, breathed and spoke. He was obliged by obedience to account to his superior, Father Louis Pinheyro, all that had passed in him after the last pangs of his agony; and here is the summary of the relation which he wrote with his own hand: "First, I saw from my death-bed,' he says, "my Father, St. Ignatius, accompanied by some of our Fathers in heaven, who was coming to visit his sick children, seeking those who seemed worthy to be presented to our Lord. When he was near me

I thought for an instant that he might take me, and my heart leaped with joy; but he soon described to me what I must correct before obtaining so great a favor."

Then, however, by a mysterious dispensation of Providence, the soul of Brother Pereyra was momentarily released from his body, and immediately the sight of the hideous troop of demons, rushing headlong upon him, filled him with dread. But, at the same time, his angel-guardian and St. Anthony of Padua, his countryman and patron, put his enemies to flight, and invited him in their company to take a momentary glimpse and taste of something of the joys and pains of eternity. "They then, by turns, led me to a place of delights, where they showed mean incomparable crown of glory, but one which I had not yet merited; then, to the brink of the abysmal pit, where I beheld souls accursed falling into the everlasting fire, as thick as grains of corn, cast beneath an ever-turning millstone. The infernal pit was like one of these limekilns, in which the flame is smothered for an instant beneath the heap of materials thrown into it, only to fire up again by the fuel with a more frightful violence."

Led thence to the tribunal of the Sovereign Judge, Antony Pereyra heard his sentence to the fire of purgatory, and nothing here below, he declares, could give an idea of what is suffered there, or of the state of anguish to which the soul is reduced by the desire and postponement of the enjoyment of God and of His blessed presence.

So when, by our Lord's command, his soul was united again to his body, neither the new tortures of sickness, which, for six entire months, combined with the daily help of iron and fire, caused his flesh, irremediably attacked by the corruption of this first death to waste away; nor the frightful penances to which, so far as obedience allowed him, he never ceased to subject himself for the forty-six years of his new life, were able to quench his thirst for sufferings and expiation. "All this," he used to say, "is nothing to what the justice and mercy of God have caused me, not only to see, but to endure." Finally, as an authentic seal of so many wonders, Brother Pereyra detailed to his Superior the hidden designs of Providence on the future restoration of the Kingdom of Portugal, at that time still distant nearly half a century. But it may be fearlessly added that the most unexceptionable avouchment of all these prodigies was the surprising sanctity to which Antony Pereyra never ceased for a single day to rise.

III. APPARITIONS OF THE DAMNED

St. Antoninus, Archbishop of Florence, relates, in his writings, a terrible fact which, about the middle of the fifteenth century, spread fright over the whole North of Italy. A young man of good stock, who, at the age of 16 or 17, had had the misfortune of concealing a mortal sin in confession, and, in that state, of receiving Communion, had put off from week to week, month to month, the painful disclosure of his sacrileges. Tortured by remorse, instead of discovering with simplicity his misfortune, he sought to gain quiet by great penances, but to no purpose. Unable to bear the strain any longer, he entered a monastery; there, at least, he said to himself, I will tell all, and expiate my frightful sins. Unhappily, he was most welcomed as a holy young man by his superiors, who knew him by reputation, and his shame again got the better of him. Accordingly, he deferred his confession of this sin to a later period; and a year, two years, three years, passed in this deplorable state; he never dared to reveal his misfortune. Finally, sickness seemed to him to afford an easy means of doing it. "Now is the time," he says to himself; "I am going to tell all; I will make a general confession before I die." But this time, instead of frankly and fairly declaring his faults, he twisted them so artfully that his confessor was unable to understand him. He hope to come back again the next day: an attack of delirium came on, and the unfortunate man died.

The community, who were ignorant of the frightful reality, were full of veneration for the deceased. His body was borne with a certain degree of solemnity into the church of the monastery, and lay exposed in the choir until the next morning when the funeral was to be celebrated.

A few moments before the time fixed for the ceremony, one of the Brothers, sent to toll the bell, saw before him, all of a sudden, the deceased, encompassed by chains, that seemed aglow with fire, while something blazing appeared all over his person. Frightened, the poor Brother fell on his knees, with his eyes riveted on the terrifying apparition. Then the damned soul said to him: "*Do not pray for me, I am in here for all eternity;*" and he related the sad story of his false shame and sacrileges. Thereupon, he vanished, leaving in the church a disgusting odor, which spread all over the monastery, as if to prove the truth of all the Brother just saw and heard. Notified at once, the Superiors had the corpse taken away, deeming it unworthy of ecclesiastical burial.

After having cited the preceding example, Monsignor de Segur adds what follows [Opuscule on Hell]:

"In our century, three facts of the same kind, more authentic than some others have come to my knowledge. The first happened almost in my family.

"It was in Russia, at Moscow, a short while before the horrible campaign of 1812. My maternal grandfather, Count Rostopchine, the Military Governor of Moscow, was very intimate with General Count Orloff, celebrated for his bravery, but as godless as he was brave.

"One day, at the close of a supper, Count Orloff and one of his friends, General V., also a disciple of Voltaire, had set to horribly ridiculing religion, especially hell. '*Yet,*' said Orloff; '*yet if, by chance, there should be anything the other side of the curtain?*' '*Well,*' took up General V., '*whichever of us shall depart first, will come to inform the other of it. Is it agreed?*' '*An excellent idea,*' replied Count Orloff; and both interchanged very seriously their word of honor not to miss the engagement.

"A few weeks later, one of those great wars which Napoleon had the gift of creating at that time, burst forth. The Russian army began the campaign, and

General V. received orders to start out forthwith to take an important command.

"He had left Moscow about two or three weeks, when one morning, at a very early hour, while my grandfather was dressing, his chamber door is rudely pushed open. It was Count Orloff, in dressing-gown and slippers, his hair on end, his eye wild, and pale like a dead man. *'What, Orloff, you? at this hour? and in such a costume? What ails you? what has happened?' 'My dear,'* replies Count Orloff, *'I believe I am beside myself. I have just seen General V.' 'Has General V., then, come back?' 'Well, no,'* rejoins Orloff, throwing himself on a sofa, and holding his head between his hands; *'no, he has not come back, and that is what frightens me!'*

My grandfather did not understand him. He tried to soothe him. *"Relate to me,"* he says to Orloff, *"what has happened you, and what all this means."* Then, striving to stifle his emotion, the Count related the following: "My dear Rostopchine, some time ago, V. and I mutually swore that the first of us who died should come and tell the other if there is anything on the other side of the curtain. Now, this morning, scarcely half an hour since, I was calmly lying awake in my bed, not thinking at all of my friend, when, all of a sudden, the curtains of my bed were rudely parted, and at two steps from me I see General V. standing up, pale, with his right hand on his breast, and saying to me: *'There is a hell, and I am there!'* and he disappeared. I came at once to you. My head is splitting! What a strange thing! I do not know what to think about it."

My grandfather calmed him as well as he could. It was no easy matter. He spoke of hallucinations, nightmares; perhaps he was asleep... There are many extraordinary unaccountable things... and other common-places, which constitute the comfort of freethinkers. Then he ordered his carriage, and took Count Orloff back to his hotel.

Now, ten or twelve days after this strange incident, an army messenger brought my grandfather among other news, that of the death of General V. The very morning of the day, Count Orloff had seen and heard him, the same hour he appeared at Moscow, the unfortunate General, reconnoitering the enemy's position, had been shot through the breast by a bullet, and had fallen stark dead.

"There is a hell, and I am there!" these are the words of one who came back.

Mgr. de Segur relates a second fact, which he regards as alike free from doubt, He had learned it in 1859, of a most honorable priest, and Superior of an important community. This priest had the particulars of it from a near relation of the lady of whom it had happened. At that time, Christmas Day, 1859, this person was still living, and little over forty years.

She chanced to be in London in the winter of 1847-48. She was a widow, about twenty-nine years old, quite rich and worldly. Among the gallants who frequented her *salon,* there was noticed a young lord, whose attentions compromised her extremely, and whose conduct, besides, was anything but edifying!

One evening, or rather one night, for it was close upon midnight, she was reading in her bed some novel, coaxing sleep. One o'clock struck by the clock; she blew out her taper. She was about to fall asleep when, to her great astonishment, she noticed that a strange, wan glimmer of light, which seemed to come from the door of the drawing-room, spread by degrees into her chamber, and increased momentarily. Stupefied at first, and not knowing what this meant, she began to get alarmed, when she saw the drawing-room door slowly open and the young lord, the partner of her disorders, entered her room. Before she had time to say a single word, he seized her by the left wrist, and with a hissing voice, syllabled to her in English: *"There is a hell!"* The pain she felt in her arm was so great that she lost her senses.

When, half an hour after, she came to again, she rang for her chamber-maid. The latter, on entering felt a keen smell of burning. Approaching her mistress, who could hardly speak, she noticed on her wrist so deep a burn, that the bone was laid bare, and the flesh almost consumed; this burn was the size of a man's hand. Moreover, she remarked that, from the door of the saloon to the bed, and from the bed to that same door, the carpet bore the imprint of a man's steps, which had burned through the stuff. By the directions of her mistress, she opened the drawing-room door: there, more traces were seen on the carpet outside.

The following day, the unhappy lady learned with a terror easy to be divined that, on that very night, about one o'clock in the morning, her lord had been found dead drunk under the table, that his servants had carried him to his room, and that there he had died in their arms.

I do not know, added the Superior, whether that terrible lesson converted the unfortunate lady, but what I do know, is that she is still alive, and that to conceal from the sight the traces of her ominous burn, she wears on the left wrist, like a bracelet, a wide gold band, which she does not take off day or night. I repeat it, I have all these details from her near relation, a serious Christian, in whose word I repose the fullest belief. They are never spoken of, even in the family; and I only confide them to you, suppressing every proper name.

Notwithstanding the disguise beneath which this apparition has been, and must be enveloped, it seems to me impossible, adds Mgr. de Segur, to call in doubt the dreadful authenticity of the details.

Here is a third fact related by the same writer. In the year 1873, he writes, a few days before the Assumption, occurred again one of these apparitions from beyond the grave, which so efficaciously confirm the reality of hell. It was in Rome. A brothel, opened in that city after the Piedmontese invasion, stood near a police station. One of the bad girls who lived there had been wounded in the hand, and it was found necessary to take her to hospital of CONSOLATION. Whether her blood, vitiated by bad living, had brought on mortification of wound, or from an unexpected complication, she died suddenly during the night. At the same instant, one of her companions, who surely was ignorant of what had just happened at the hospital, began to utter shrieks of despair to point of awaking the inhabitants of the locality, creating a flurry among the wretched creatures of the house, and provoking the intervention of the police. The dead girl of the hospital, surrounded by flames, had appeared to her, and said: "*I am damned! and if you do not wish to be like me, leave this place of infamy and return to God.*"

Nothing could quell the despair of this girl, who, at daybreak, departed, leaving the whole house plunged in a stupor, especially as soon as the death of her companion at the hospital was known.

Just at this period, the mistress of the place, an exalted Garribaldian, and known as such by brethren and friends, fell sick. She soon sent for a priest to receive the sacraments. The ecclesiastical authority deputed for thus task, a worthy prelate, Mgr. Sirolli, the pastor of the parish of Saint-Saviour *in Laura*. He, fortified by special instructions, presented himself, and exacted of the sick woman, before all, in the presence of many witnesses, the full and entire retractation of her blasphemies against the Sovereign Pontiff, and the discontinuance of the infamous trade she plied. The unhappy creature did so without hesitating, consented to purge her house, then made her confession and received the holy Viaticum with great sentiments of repentance and humility.

Feeling that she was dying, she besought, with tears, the good pastor not to leave her, frightened as she always was by the apparition of that damned girl. Mgr. Sirolli, unable to satisfy her on account of the proprieties which would not permit him to spend the night in such a place, sent to the police for two men, closed up the house, and remained until the dying woman had breathed her last.

Pretty soon, all Rome became acquainted with the details of these tragic occurrences. As ever, the ungodly and lewd ridiculed them, taking good care not to seek for any information about them; the good profited by them, to become still better and more faithful to their duties.

IV. THE DENIAL OF HELL IS FOOLISH BRAVADO

There are some miserable men, let us rather say, fools, who, in the delirium of their iniquity, make bold to declare that they laugh at hell. They say so, but only with their lips; their consciences protest and give them the lie. Collot de Herbois, famous for his impiety as much as for is sanguinary ferocity, was the chief author of the massacres of Lyons, in 1793; he caused the destruction of 1,600 victims. Six years after, in 1799, he was banished to Cayenne, and used to give vent to his infernal rage by blaspheming the holiest things. The least act of religion, became the subject of his jests. Having seen a soldier make the sign of the cross, *"Imbecile!"* he said to him. *"You still believe in superstition! Do you not know that God, the Holy Virgin, Paradise, Hell, are the inventions of the accursed tribe of priests?"* Shortly after he fell sick and was seized by violent pains. In an access of fever he swallowed, at a single draught, a bottle of liquor. His disease increased; he felt as if burned by a fire that was devouring his bowels. He uttered frightful shrieks, called upon God, the Holy Virgin, a priest, to come to his relief. *"Well, indeed,"* said the soldier to him, *"you ask for a priest? You fear hell then? You used to curse the priests, make fun of hell! Alas!"* He then answered: *"My tongue was lying to my heart."* Pretty soon, he expired, vomiting blood and foam.

The following incident happened in 1837. A young under-lieutenant, being in Paris, entered the Church of the Assumption, near the Toilers, and saw a priest kneeling near a confessional. As he made religion the habitual subject of his jokes, he wished to go to confession to while away the time, and went into the confessional. "Monsieur l'abbé," he said, "would you be good enough to hear my confession?" "Willingly my son; confess unrestrained." "But I must first say that I am a rather unique kind of a sinner." "No matter; the sacrament of penance has been instituted for all sinners." "But I am not very much of a believer in religious matters." "You believe more than you think." "Believe? I? I am a regular scoffer." The confessor saw with whom he had to deal, and that there was some mystification. He replied, smiling: "You are a regular scoffer? Are you then making fun of me too?" The pretended penitent smiled in like manner. "Listen," the priest went on, "what you have just done here is not serious. Let us leave confession aside; and, if you please, have a little chat. I like military people greatly; and, then, you have the appearance of a good, amiable youth. Tell me, what is your rank?" "Under-lieutenant." "Will you remain an under-lieutenant long?" "Two, three, perhaps four years." "And after?" "I shall hope to become a lieutenant?" "And after?" "I hope to become a captain." "And after?" "Lieutenant-colonel?" "How old will you be then?" "Forty to forty-five years." "And after that?" "I shall become a brigadier general." "And after?" "If I rise higher, I shall be general of a division." "And after?" "After! there is nothing more except the Marshal's baton; but my pretensions do not reach so high." "Well and good. But do you intend to get married?" "Yes, when I shall be a superior officer." "Well! There you are married; a superior officer, a general, perhaps even a French marshal, who knows? And after?" "After? Upon my word, I do not know what will be after."

"See, how strange it is!" said the abbé. Then, in a tone of voice that grew more sober: "You know all that shall happen up to that point, and you do not know what will be after. Well, I know, and I am going to tell you, After, you shall die, be judged, and, if you continue to live as you do, you shall be damned, you shall go and burn in hell; that is what will be after."

As the under-lieutenant, dispirited at this conclusion, seemed anxious to steal away: "One moment, sir," said the abbé. "You are a man of honor. So am I. Agree that you have offended me, and owe me an apology. It will be simple. For eight days, before retiring to rest, you will say: 'One day I shall die; but I laugh at the idea. After my death I shall be judged; but I laugh at the idea. After my judgment, I shall be damned; but I laugh at the idea. I shall burn forever in hell; but I laugh at the idea!' That is all. But you are going to give me your word of honor not to neglect it, eh?"

More and more wearied, and wishing, at any price, to extricate himself from this false step, the under-lieutenant made the promise. In the evening, his word being given, he began to carry out his promise. *"I shall die,"* he says. *"I shall be judged."* He had not the courage to add: *"I laugh at the idea."* The week had not passed before he returned to the Church of the Assumption, made his confession seriously, and came out of the confessional his face bathed with tears, and with joy in his heart.

A young person who had become an unbeliever in consequence of his dissipation, kept incessantly shooting sarcasm at religion, and making jests of its most awful truths. *"Juliette,"* some one said to her one day, *"this will end badly. God will be tired of your blasphemies, and you shall be punished."* *"Bah,"* she answered insolently. *"It gives me very little trouble. Who has returned from the other world to relate what passes there?"* Less than eight days after she was found in her room, giving no sign of life, and already cold. As there was no doubt that she was dead, she was put in a coffin and buried. The following day, the grave-digger, digging a new grave beside that of the unhappy Juliette, heard some noise, it seemed to him that there was a knocking in the adjoining coffin. At once, he puts his ear to the ground, and in fact hears a smothered voice, crying out: "Help! help!" The authorities were summoned; by their orders, the grave was opened, the coffin taken up and unnailed. The shroud is removed; there is no further doubt, Juliette was buried alive. Her hair, her shroud were in disorder, and her face was streaming with blood. While they are releasing her, and feeling her heart to be assured that it still beats, she heaves a sigh, like a person for a long time deprived of air; then she opens her eyes, makes an effort to lift herself up, and says: *"My God, I thank thee."* Afterward, when she had got her senses well back, and by the aid of some food, recovered her strength, she added: *"When I regained consciousness in the grave and recognized the frightful reality of my burial, when after having uttered shrieks, I endeavored to break my coffin, and struck my forehead against the boards, I saw that all was useless; death appeared to me with all its horrors; it was less the bodily than the eternal death that frightened me. I saw I was going to be damned. My God, I had but too well deserved it! Then I prayed, I shouted for help, I lost consciousness again, until I awoke above ground. O, goodness of my God!"* she said, again shedding tears, *"I had despised the truths of faith; thou hast punished me, but in thy mercy, I am converted and repentant."*

They who deny hell will be forced to admit it soon; but alas! it will be too late. Father Nieremberg, in his work *Difference between Time and Eternity,* speaks of an unfortunate sinner, who, as the result of his evil ways, had lost the faith. His virtuous wife exhorted him to return to God, and reminded him of hell, but he would answer, obstinately: *"There is no hell."* One day his wife found him dead, and, strange circumstance, he held in his hand a mysterious paper, on which, in large characters, was traced this terrifying avowal: *"I now know that there is a hell!"*

V. AWAKENING OF THE UNGODLY SOUL IN HELL

Unhappy sinners, who are lulled to rest by the illusions of the world, and who live as if there was no hell, will be suddenly stripped of their illusions by the most frightful of catastrophes. From the midst of their pleasures they shall fall into the pit of torments.

The disaster of the Cafe Kivoto supplies an image of the catastrophe, still more terrible, which awaits them, soon or late.

The Kivoto was a theatrical cafe at Smyrna, built upon piles in the sea. The extremely stout stakes that kept the house above the waves, water and time-eaten, had lost their solid contents. It was on the 11th of February, 1873, at 10 o'clock P.M. Two hundred persons had assembled to witness a comic spectacle. They were amusing themselves, when, all at once, a frightful crash was heard. At the same moment everything gave way and was turned topsy-turvy; the house, with the theatre and spectators, was pitched forward and swallowed up in the sea. What an awful surprise for these amusement amateurs! A more tragical surprise awaits the worldling. A day will come when from the centre of his pleasure, he shall, all of a sudden, behold himself cast headlong into a sea of sulfur and fire.

On the night of the 31st of March--1st of April, 1873, a stately and magnificent steamship, the *Atlantic,* foundered on the Canadian banks, near Halifax. The number on board, passengers and crew, reached 950, of whom 700 were lost in this shipwreck. Most of them were wrapped in sleep, when the vessel, striking some rocks, sank almost instantaneously. Swallowed up by the sea in the middle of their repose, they awoke in the waters, and were suffocated before being able to account for the terrible accident which had just happened. Frightful awaking! But more frightful will be the awaking of the atheist when he shall see himself suddenly engulfed in hell.

On the 28th of December, 1879, occurred the Tay bridge accident. The train from London to Edinburgh crosses the Tay, near Dundee, over an iron bridge half a league long. A dreadful storm, which had swelled the waves and broken the bridge during the day, ended by sweeping away several arches, despite the iron cross-bars piers. These arches, when falling, left an empty space, which was not perceived in the darkness. At 7:30 P.M. the express train out from Edinburgh thunders along, carrying a hundred travelers; it mounts the fatal bridge, and soon, coming on the empty space, is hurled into the waves. Not a cry was heard; in the twinkling of an eye the victims were in the depths below. What a surprise! what a sudden change! But what will it be when the sinner shall see himself, in the twinkling of an eye, in the pit of hell?

VI. TRUTH OF HELL

This is how the Son of God speaks to us of hell:

"Woe to the world because of scandals; for it must needs be that scandals come; nevertheless, woe to that man by whom scandal cometh!"

"If, then, thy hand or thy foot scandalize thee, cut it off and cast it from thee; it is better for thee to go into life maimed or lame, than, having two hands or two feet, be cast into everlasting fire."

"And if thy eye scandalize thee, pluck it out and cast it from thee; it is better for thee, having one eye, to enter into life, than, having two eyes, to be cast into hell fire." (*Matt.* xviii, 7; compare v., 29)

"And fear ye not them that kill the body, and are not able to kill the soul; but rather fear him that can destroy both soul and body into hell." (*Matt.* x. 28)

"The rich man also died, and he was buried in hell."

"Now, lifting up his eyes when he was in torments, he saw Abraham afar off, and Lazarus in his bosom."

"And he said: Father Abraham, have mercy on me, and send Lazarus, that he may dip the tip of his finger in water to cool my tongue, for I am tormented in this flame." (*Luke* xvi., 22)

"Then the Judge will say to them that shall be on his left hand: Depart from me, you cursed, into everlasting fire, which was prepared for the devil and his angels." (*Matt* xxv., 41)

"Many shall come from the east and the west, and shall sit down in the kingdom of heaven.

"But the children of the kingdom shall be cast out into the exterior darkness: there shall be weeping and gnashing of teeth." (*Matt.* viii., 11)

"The King went in to see the guests, and he saw there a man who had not on a wedding garment.

"And he saith to him: Friend, how camest thou in hither, not having on a wedding garment? But he was silent.

"Then the King said to the waiters: Bind his hands and feet, and cast him into the exterior darkness: there shall weeping, and gnashing of teeth." (*Matt. v., 22)*

"The unprofitable servant cast ye out into the exterior darkness: there shall be weeping, and gnashing of teeth." (*Matt* xxv., 30)

"But I say to you: Whosoever is angry with his brother shall be in danger of the judgment, and whosoever shall say to his brother, Thou fool, shall be in danger of hell fire." (*Matt.* v., 22)

"The Son of Man shall send His angels, and they shall gather out of His Kingdom all scandals and them that work iniquity;

"And shall cast them into the furnace of fire; there shall be weeping and gnashing of teeth." (*Matt.* xiii., 41)

"If thy hand scandalize thee, cut it off; it is better for thee to enter into life maimed, than having two hands to go into hell, into unquenchable fire.

"There, the gnawing worm dies not and the fire is not extinguished.

"And if thy foot scandalize thee, cut it off; it is better for thee to enter lame into life everlasting than having two feet, to be cast into the hell of unquenchable fire.

"Where their worm dieth not, and the fire is not extinguished.

"And if thy eye scandalize thee, pluck it out; it is better for thee with one eye to enter into the

Kingdom of God, than, having two eyes, to be cast into the hell of fire.

"Where their worm dieth not, and the fire is not extinguished." (*Mark* ix., 42)

"Every tree that bringeth not forth good fruit, shall be cut down and shall be cast into the fire." (*Matt.* XII., 19)

"I am the vine; you the branches; he that abideth in Me, and I in him, the same beareth much fruit.

"If any one abide not in Me, he shall be cast forth as a branch, and shall wither, and they shall gather him up, and cast him into the fire, and he burneth." (*John* xv., 5)

"Daughters of Jerusalem, weep not over Me, but weep for yourselves and for your children.

"For the days shall come, wherin they shall say to the mountains: Fall upon us; and to the hills: Cover us.

"For if in the green wood they do these things, what shall be done in the dry? -- that is to say, what will sinners be, destined, like the dry wood, to be burned." *(Luke xxiii., 31)*

"Already, the axe is laid to the root of the tree: and every tree that doth not yield good fruit, shall be cut down and cast into the fire.

"He that shall come after Me is mightier than I, and he shall baptize you in the Holy Ghost and fire.

"Whose fan is in his hand and he will thoroughly cleanse his floor; and gather his wheat into the barn, but the chaff he will burn with unquenchable fire." Words of St. John the Baptist. *(Matt. iii., 10.)*

"The beast and the false prophet who had seduced them who had received the character of the beast, and who had admired his image, were cast alive into the pool of fire burning with brimstone." (*Apoc.,* xix., 20.)

"Where they were tormented day and night, for ever and ever.

"And whosoever was not found written in the book of life, was cast into the pool of fire." (*Apoc. xx.,* 15)

To doubt about hell, is to doubt the infallible word of God; it is to give ear to the speech of the libertines rather than to the infallible teaching of the Church. The Church teaches that there is a hell; a libertine tells you that there is not; and should you prefer to believe a libertine? An honorable Roman,

Emilius Scaurus, was accused by a certain Varus, a man without word or honor. Being obliged to prove his innocence, Scaurus addressed the people in this short speech: "*Romans, you know Varus says I am guilty of the crime charged against me, and I protest that I am not guilty. Varus says yes, I say no; whom do you believe?*

The people applauded, and the accuser was confounded.

Natural reason confirms the dogma of hell. An atheist was boasting that he did not believe in hell. Among his hearers, there was a sensible young man, modest, but who thought that he ought to shut the silly speaker's mouth. He put him a single question: "*Sir,*" he said, "*the kings of the earth have prisons to punish their refractory subjects; how can God, the King of the Universe, be without a prison for those who outrage His majesty?*" The sinner had not a word to answer. The appeal was presented to the light of his own reason, which proclaims that, if kings have prisons, God must have a hell.

The atheist who denies hell is like the thief who should deny the prison. A thief was threatened with sentence to prison. The foolish fellow replied: "*There is no Court, there is no prison.*" He was speaking thus, when an officer of justice put his hand on his shoulder, and dragged him before the Judge. This is an image of the atheist who is foolish enough to deny hell. A day will come, when, taken unawares by divine justice, he shall see himself dashed headlong into the pit which he stubbornly denied, and he shall be forced to acknowledge the terrible reality.

The atheist who denies hell is like the African heron. That stupid bird, when chased by hunters, plunges its head into the sand, and keeping stirless, believes it is secure from danger, because it does not see the enemy. But soon the piercing arrow comes to undeceive it. Thus absorbed, sunk in earthly things, the sinner is persuaded that he has nothing to fear from hell until the day when death strikes him and shows him, by a sad experience, how deceive he has been.

The truth of hell is so clearly revealed that heresy has never denied it. Protestants, who have demolished almost all dogmas, have not dared to touch this dogma. This fact suggests to a Catholic lady this witty answer. Anxiously importuned by two Protestant ministers to pass over into the camp of the Reformation: "*Gentlemen,*" she replied, "*you have indeed achieved a fine reformation. You have suppressed fasting, confession, purgatory. Unfortunately, you have kept hell; put hell away, and I shall be one of you.*" Yes, Messrs.

Freethinkers, remove hell, and then ask us to be yours. But know that an "*I do not believe in it,*" is not sufficient to do away with it.

Is it not the most inconceivable folly to rely on a *perhaps,* at the risk of falling into hell? Two atheists went one day into an anchorite's cell. At the sight of his instruments of penance, they asked him why he was leading so mortified a life. *"To deserve paradise,"* he replied. *"Good Father,"* they said, smiling, "*You would be nicely caught, if there is nothing after death!"* "*Gentlemen,"* rejoined the holy man, as he looked at them with compassion, *"you will be quite otherwise, if there is any."*

A young man belonging to a Catholic family in Holland, as a consequence of imprudent reading, had the misfortune to lose the treasure of faith and fall into a state of complete indifference. It was a subject of the bitterest grief for his parents, especially his pious mother. In vain did this other Monica give him the most solid lectures, in vain did she admonish him with tears to come back to God; her unhappy son was deaf and insensible. Yet, at last, to satisfy his mother, he was pleased to consent to spend a few days in a religious house, there to follow the exercises of a retreat, or rather, as he put it, to rest a few days and smoke tobacco, an enjoyment he loved. So, he listened with a distracted mind to the instructions given to those making the retreat, and speedily after began again to smoke without thinking further of what he had heard. The instruction on hell, to which he seemed to listen to like the rest, came on, but being back again in his little cell, while he was taking his smoke as usual, a reflection arose, in spite of him, in his mind. *"If, however, it should be true,"* he says to himself, "*that there is a hell! If there be one, clearly it shall be for me! And in reality, do I know, myself, that there is not a hell? I am obliged to acknowledge that I have no certainty in this behalf; the whole ground of my ideas is only a perhaps. Now, to run the risk of burning for eternity on a perhaps, frankly speaking, as a matter of extravagance, would be to go beyond the bounds. If there are some who have such courage, I have not sufficiently lost my senses to imitate them."* Thereupon, he begins to pray, grace penetrates his soul, his doubts vanish, he rises up, converted.

A pious author relates the history of the tragic punishment that befell an ungodly scoffer of hell. This was a man of quality, whom the author, through respect for his family, does not name; he designates him by the fictitious name of Leontius. This unfortunate man made it a boast to brave heaven and hell, which he treated as chimerical superstitions. One day, when a feast was about to be celebrated at his castle, he took a walk, accompanied by a friend, and wished to go through the cemetery. Chancing to stumble against a skull lying on the ground, he kicked it aside with profane, blasphemous words: *"Out of my way,"* he said, "*rotten bones, worthless remains of what is not more."* His companion, who did not share in his sentiments, ventured to say to him *"that he did wrong to use this language. The remains of the dead,"* he added, *"must be respected, on account of their souls, which are always alive, and which will assume their bodies again on the day of the resurrection."* Leontius answered by this challenge spoken to the skull: *"If the spirit that animated thee still exists, let it come and tell me some news about the other world. I invite it for this very evening to my banquet."* Evening came, he was at table with numerous friends, and telling his adventure of the cemetery, while repeating his profanations, when, all at once, a great noise is made and almost at the same time a horrible ghost appears in the dining-room, and spreads fright among the guests, Leontius, especially, losing all audacity, is pale, trembling, out of his wits. he wants to flee; the specter does not give him time, but springs on him with the swiftness of lightning, and smashed his head to pieces against the wainscot. I do not know how far this recital is authentic; but what is certain is that a day will come when the pride of the ungodly shall be dashed down, and their heads broken by the Judge of the living and the dead: *"The Lord shall judge among nations, He shall fill ruins; He shall crush the heads in the land of many."* (Ps. 109.)

Here is another fact almost contemporaneous and related by a trustworthy author: Two young men, whose names, through respect for their families, must remain secret, but whom I shall call Eugene and Alexander, old schoolmates and college friends, met again later in life after a long separation. Eugene, having stayed at home; used to occupy himself with the works of charity, according to the spirit of the Society of St. Vincent de Paul, of which he was a member. Alexander had entered the army and obtained the rank of colonel; but, unhappily, there lost every spark of religion. Having procured a leave of absence of a few days, he had returned to his family, and wished to see Eugene. The interview happened on a Sunday. After they had chatted together for a time, "*Friend,*" said Eugene, *"it is time to leave you. Wither do you wish to go? It cannot be there is anything pressing?" "I am going first after the business of salvation; then I must attend a benevolent reunion." "Poor Eugene; I see it; you still believe in paradise and hell. 'Tis all a chimera, superstition, fanaticism." "Dear Alexander, do not speak so; you, like me, learned that the dogmas of faith rest on unexceptionable facts."* *"Chimeras, I tell you, which I believe no longer. If there be a hell, I am willing to go there today. Come with me to the theatre."* *"Dear friend, use your liberty, but do not brave God's justice."* Eugene spoke to a deaf man, who was unwilling to heed salutary advice. He left him with a sore heart. That very day, in the evening, Eugene was already in bed, when he was awakened. *"Quick,"* they said to him, *"rise, go to Alexander's; he has been just brought back from the theatre, seized by a frightful pain."* Eugene runs thither, and finds him tossed by violent convulsions, with foam in his mouth and rolling his wild eyes. As soon as he sees Eugene, *"You say there is a hell,"* he shouts; *"you say, truly, there is a hell, and I am going thither; I am there already; I fell its tortures and fury."*

In vain did Eugene try to calm him; the unhappy man answers only by yells and blasphemies. In the transports of his rage, he tore with his teeth the flesh off his arms, and cast the bleeding fragments at Eugene, his mother, and sisters. It was in this paroxysm of agony that he expired. His mother died of grief, his two sisters entered religion, and Eugene also quitted the world; owner of a brilliant fortune, he forsook all to consecrate himself to God, and avoid hell.

VII. THE PAINS OF HELL

What predominates in the words of Scripture when it exhibits to us the pains of Hell is the terrible torture of the fire. The Scriptures call Hell a "pool of sulphur and fire," the gehenna of fire," the eternal fire," a "fiery furnace where the fire shall never be extinguished." But this fire, kindled by divine justice, will possess an activity incomparably superior to that of all the furnaces, all the fires, of this world. Alas! Do we understand how it shall be possible to bear it? How it will be necessary to dwell in it as in an everlasting habitation? "Which of you," demands the Prophet, "can dwell with devouring fire? Which of you shall bear everlasting burnings?" (Isaias 33:14).

In 1604, in the city of Brussels, there occurred the celebrated apparition of a damned soul, attested by Blessed Richard of St. Ann, of the Order of St. Francis, who suffered martyrdom at Nagasaki, in Japan, on September 10, 1622. Blessed Richard related the fact to a theologian of the Spanish Inquisition, Father Alphonsus of Andrada, of the Company of Jesus; he, in turn, communicated it to Adrian Lyroeus, who has inserted it in his Trisagium Marianum, Book III. Saint Alphonsus Liguori, who cites the same fact in his Glories of

Mary, has made Blessed Richard one of the two actors in this frightful drama; he (Bl. Richard) was only a witness, like many others who were living at Brussels, but the impression he experienced was so lively that it became the determining cause of his entrance into the Seraphic order.

This is how the occurrence is related, after authentic documents in the Annals of Franciscan Missions, for the years 1866-67. It was not without a terrible, though merciful interposition of God's justice, that Blessed Richard was brought to demand the habit of St. Francis. It was in 1604. There were at Brussels, where Richard was at that time, two young students who, instead of applying themselves to study, thought only of how to live in pleasure and dissipation. One night, among others, when they had gone to indulge in sin in a house of ill-fame, one of the two left the place after some time, leaving his miserable companion behind him.

Having reached home, he was about to lie down in bed, when he remembered that he had not recited that day the few Hail Marys which he had the habit of saying every day in honour of the Holy Virgin. As he was overpowered by sleep, it was troublesome for him; however, he made an effort and said them, although without devotion; then he went to bed. In his first sleep he heard all of a sudden, a rude knocking at the door; and immediately afterward he saw before him his companion, disfigured and hideous.

"Who are you?" he said to him. "What? Don't you know me?" replied the unhappy youth. "But how are you so changed? You look like a devil?" "Ah, pity me; I am damned!" "How is that?" "Well, know that upon leaving that accursed house a devil sprang upon me and strangled me. My body has remained in the middle of the street, and my soul is in Hell. Know, moreover, that the same chastisement awaited you, but the Virgin preserved you from it, thanks to your practice of reciting every day a few Hail Marys in her honour. Happy are you if you know how to profit by this information, which the Mother of God gives you through me."

While finishing these words, the damned soul partly opened his garment, allowed the flames and serpents that were tormenting him to be seen, and vanished. Then the young man, melting into tears, threw himself on his face on the floor to thank the Holy Virgin Mary, his deliverer. Now, while he was praying in this manner and reflecting upon what he ought to do to change his life, he heard the Matins bell ring at the Franciscan Monastery.

That very moment he cried out, "There it is that God calls me to do penance." The next day indeed, at a very early hour, he went to the monastery and begged the Father Guardian to receive him. The Father, who was aware of his bad life, having presented difficulties at first, the young student, shedding a torrent of tears, related to him all that had taken place. And really, two religious, having repaired to the street indicated, found the corpse of the wretched youth, black as a coal. Then the postulant was admitted among the Brothers, whom he edified by a life altogether devoted to penance.

Such is the terrible fact which struck dismay and fright into many souls and which induced Blessed Richard also to consecrate himself entirely to God in the same Order into which the young student, so wonderfully protected by Mary, had just been received.

The following fact is related by Father Martin del Rio, from the Annals of the Company of Jesus. It is an apparition that occurred in 1590 and was vouched for by trustworthy witnesses: Not far from Lima, dwelt a Christian lady who had three maid-servants, one of whom, called Martha, was a young Indian of about sixteen years. Martha was a Christian, but little by little she grew cool in the devotion she had at first displayed, became negligent in her prayers, and light, coquettish, and wanton in her conversations. Having fallen dangerously ill, she received the Last Sacraments. After this serious ceremony, during which she had evinced very little piety, she said, smiling to her two fellow servants, that in the confession she had just made she had taken good care not to tell all her sins to the priest. Frightened by this language, the girls reported it to their mistress, who by dint of exhortations and threats, obtained from the sick girl a sign of repentance and the promise to make a sincere and Christian confession. Martha confessed then, over again, and died shortly afterward.

Scarcely had she breathed her last, when her corpse emitted an extraordinary and intolerable stench. They were obliged to remove it from the house to a shed. The dog in the courtyard, usually a quiet animal, howled piteously, as if he were undergoing torture. After the interment, the lady, according to custom, was dining in the garden in the open air, when a heavy stone fell suddenly onto the centre of the table with a horrible crash and caused all the table settings to bounce, but without breaking any article. One of the servants, having occupied the room in which Martha had died, was awakened by frightful noises; all the furniture seemed to be moved by an invisible force and thrown to the floor.

We understand how the servant did not continue to occupy that room; her companion ventured to take her place, but the same scenes were renewed. Then they agreed to spend the night together there. This time they distinctly heard Martha's voice, and soon that wretched girl appeared before them in the most horrible state, and all on fire. She said that by God's command she had come to reveal her condition to them, that she was damned for her sins of impurity and for the sacrilegious confessions she had continued to make until death. She added, "Tell what I have just revealed to you, that others may profit by my misfortune." At these words she uttered a despairing cry and disappeared.

The fire of Hell is a real fire, a fire that burns like this world's fire, although it is infinitely more active. Must not there be a real fire in Hell, seeing that there is a real fire in Purgatory? "It is the same fire," says St. Augustine, "that tortures the damned and purifies the elect."

A number of indisputable facts demonstrates the reality of the fire in the place of expiation. This is what Mgr. de Segur relates: "In the year 1870, in the month of April," he writes, "I saw, or at least, touched at Foligno, near Assisi, in Italy, one of those frightful imprints of fire, caused sometimes by souls that appear and prove that the fire of the other life is a real fire. On November 4, 1859, there died of a stroke of apoplexy, at the Convent of the Tertiary Franciscans of Foligno, a good Sister named Theresa Gesta, who had been many years mistress of novices and at the same time in charge of the poor little clothesroom of the convent. She was born at Corsa in Bastia in 1797, and she entered the convent in February, 1826. It need not be said that she was well prepared for death.

"Twelve days afterward on the 6th of November, a sister named Anna Felicia, who replaced her in her office, went up to the wardrobe and was about to enter, when she heard moans which seemed to come from the interior of this room. Somewhat alarmed, she hastened to open the door; no one was there. But new moans resounded, so clearly articulated that, despite her usual courage, she felt seized by fear. 'Jesus, Mary!' she exclaimed, 'what is this?' She had not finished when she heard a plaintive voice accompanied by this mournful sigh: 'Oh, my God, how I suffer!' ('Oh! Dio che peno tanto.') The shocked sister recognized at once the voice of poor Sister Theresa. Then the whole hall was filled with a dense smoke, and the ghost of

Sister Theresa appeared, moving toward the door, while gliding along by the wall. Having almost reached the door, she exclaimed forcibly: 'This is a sign of the mercy of God.' And saying that, she struck the highest panel of the door, leaving hollowed in the charred wood a most perfect stamp of her right hand; then she disappeared.

"Sister Anna Felicia had remained half dead with fear. All confused, she began to cry out and call for help. One of her companions hastened to her, then another, then the whole community; they pressed eagerly around her, and they were all astonished at finding a smell of burnt wood. Sister Anna Felicia told them what had just taken place, and showed them the terrible stamp on the door. They immediately recognized the shape of Sister Theresa's hand, which was remarkably small. Alarmed, they took flight, ran to the choir, began to pray, spent the night praying and doing penances for the deceased, and the next day all received Communion for her.

"The news spread abroad, and the different communities of the city joined their prayers to those of the Franciscans. The next day following, November 18, Sister Anna Felicia, having retired to her cell to go to bed, heard herself called by her name and recognized perfectly the voice of Sister Theresa. At the same instant an all-resplendent sphere of light appeared before her, lighting up the cell as if at noonday, and she heard Sister Theresa, who, with a joyous, triumphant voice, uttered these words: 'I died on Friday, the day of the Passion, and behold, on a Friday I depart for glory! Be brave in carrying the Cross; be courageous in suffering; love poverty.' Then, adding affectionately, 'Adieu, Adieu, Adieu!' she became transfigured into a thin, white, dazzling cloud; she flew away to Heaven and vanished.

"A canonical inquest was immediately held by the Bishop of Foligno and the magistrates of the city. On November 23, in the presence of a great number of witnesses, the grave of Sister Theresa was opened, and the stamp burned into the door was found exactly to correspond with the hand of the deceased. The result was an official judgment that established the perfect certainly and authenticity of what we have just narrated. The door with the burned mark is preserved with veneration in the Convent. The Mother Abbess, a witness of this fact, deigned to show it to me herself."

St. Peter Damian speaks of a worldling who lived only for amusement and pleasure. To no purpose was he advised to think of his soul; to no purpose was he warned that, by following the life of the wicked rich man, he should reach the same end; he continued his guilty life unto death. He had scarcely ceased to live when an anchorite (hermit) knew of his damnation. He saw him in the midst of a fiery pool; it was an immense pool like a sea, in which a great number of people, howling with despair, were plunged. They were striving to gain the shore, but it was guarded by pitiless dragons and demons, who prevented them from coming near it, and hurled them far back into that ocean of flames.

Nicholas of Nice, speaking of the fire of Hell, says that nothing on earth could give an idea of it. If, he adds, all the trees of the forests were cut down, piled up into a vast heap and set to fire, this terrible pile would not be a spark of Hell.

Vincent of Beauvais, in the 25th book of his history, narrates the following fact, which he says happened in the year 1090: Two young libertines, whether seriously or through mockery, had made a mutual promise: whichever of the two died first would come and tell the other in what state he was. So one died, and God permitted him to appear to his companion. He was in a horrible state, and seemed to be the prey of cruel sufferings, which consumed him like a burning fever and covered him with sweat. He wiped his forehead with his hand and let a drop of his sweat fall onto his friend's arm, while saying to him: "That is the sweat of Hell; you shall carry the mark of it till death." That infernal sweat burned the arm of the living man, and penetrated his flesh with unheard-of pains. He profited by this awful information and retired to a monastery.

Peter, the venerable Abbot of Cluny, tells an incident of the same kind. A dying man persisted in sin and was about to die impenitent. Burned by fever and tortured by thirst, he asked for some cold water to cool himself. God permitted, thanks to prayers offered for this wretched man, two infernal spirits to appear to him under a visible form. They bore a goblet containing a liquid, a drop of which they threw on the sick man's hand, saying: "This is the cold water used for cooling Hell!" The infernal liquid went through and through the hand, burning the flesh and bones. The attendants saw with astonishment this terrible phenomenon, as well as the convulsions of the sinner, who twisted and turned in his unspeakable sufferings. If the cold water of Hell burns like that, what will the boiling water and blazing sulphur do?

In 1870, the city of New York witnessed a conflagration, the circumstances of which offered an image of Hell. The Barnum menagerie became the prey of flames. It was stocked with tigers, lions and other wild beasts. All these animals were burned alive in their iron cages, the bars of which grew to a white heat. As the fire and the heat became more intense, the beasts became more enraged. With extreme violence they sprang at the bars of their prisons, and fell back like inert heaps, only to leap again at the insuperable obstacle which held them captive. The awful roars of the lions, the screams of the tigers, the howls of all the animals, which betrayed supreme despair, were blended together and formed a frightful chorus, bringing to mind what the damned must hear resounding in Hell. But the sounds of their terrible concert grew weaker and weaker, until the lion having uttered his last roar, the silence of death succeeded the most doleful din.

Fancy in these shining iron cages, not animals, but men, and men who, instead of dying in the fire, continue to live in it, as if their bodies were harder than iron; this would be an image of Hell, but an imperfect one, for all of that.

On Friday, February 18, 1881, there was a carnival ball given at Munich by the young artist-painters. They were numerous and masked, some as monks, priests, comical pilgrims, carrying grotesquelooking beads, and making a parody of religious usages; others like Esquimaux, covered with tow, pitch and hemp. A cigar, imprudently lighted, set fire to one of these inflammable costumes. The unfortunate person, seeing himself in flames, rushed headlong among his companions; in a minute all these tow and pitch garments were on fire. Twelve of the dancers, like living torches, ran about crazy, unable to receive help. They flung themselves onto one another, roamed around uttering mournful wails, rushed blazing into all the corners of the hall, spreading around a disgusting odor. Soon three of them were only charred corpses. Nine others died shortly after; thirteen were transported to the hospital. Among these last was Joseph Schonertzer; he expired when skillful hands were proceeding with the first bandaging. The skin peeled off his chest and arms; it came off partly in rolls, leaving the living flesh bare, scorched also by the fire. This dreadful death was regarded, not without reason, as a chastisement of the Divine Justice, which these unhappy young people had provoked by their excesses of impiety and dissipation. It presents at the same time an image of Hell, but with two great differences; it is far less cruel, and it lasts only a short time.

On March 24, 1881, a catastrophe threw the city of Nice into a state of fright and dismay; the municipal theatre became a prey to flames. This theatre had doors exceedingly narrow and absolutely insufficient for passage in case of a great rush. On March 24, a brilliant presentation, which had drawn numerous spectators, was given. The curtain had just risen for the first act when, at the expiration of a few minutes, there was an explosion among the footlights; all at once the flames were seen to issue from the frail boards and gain the stage. The shouts, "Fire! Fire!" came from all parts of the theatre, and the panic became general, especially when new explosions were heard.

The orchestra and the stage were in complete darkness. Only the glimmer of the great fire, which was rapidly spreading, revealed to the gave a few unfortunate actresses crossing the stage, crazy, wild with terror, and seeking an outlet, which the flames barred against them. The audience in the galleries, with a frenzied violence, rushed headlong down the winding starts to the corridors.

The women, the children, were trampled under foot. Only shouts of terror and despair were heard, the shouts of all those human beings, who were struggling to save their lives and who felt themselves dying, suffocated by the smoke, or ground beneath the feet of their neighbours.

When the firemen, soldiers and marines could penetrate the interior, the spectacle was horrible. There was a pile of corpses, black, hideous, some almost entirely reduced to cinders. These were the abodes of the unfortunate spectators, who rushed down, all at once, by the narrow stairways. Men, women and children, hanging on to one another, had rolled into this place. What poignant, frightful dramas must have been enacted during these few supreme minutes, when safety was possible no more. At three in the morning, 63 corpses were borne to the Church of St. Francis of Paola. They were half burned. The anguish of the most harrowing agonies might be detected in their faces and postures.

What will it be in Hell? There also, all outlet is closed in the midst of the great fire; there too, is the anguish of direct agony; but there death does not come to end it. Were these unhappy people ready to die? Alas! It is not to the theatre that we go to prepare for death! Is it not to be feared that this place may have literally been the gate of Hell for them?

On the occasion of the dreadful catastrophe of the Ring Theatre, that happened in Vienna in 1881, an estimate of the theatres burned during the previous century was made; the figure rose to several hundred. Is there not a lesson of Providence here, upholding the warning which the Church does not cease to give the faithful? Since the contemporary theatre is generally a school of irreligion and immorality, a hotbed of corruption for nations, do not the continual great fires point out sufficiently that these edifices, given up to fire, are for souls the gates of Hell?

The sight of a soul that falls into Hell is of itself alone an incomparable pain. St. Margaret Mary, as her history relates, beheld the apparition of one of her sisters in religion, recently deceased. That sister implored her prayers and suffrages; she was suffering cruelly in Purgatory. "See," she said to St. Margaret, "the bed I lie on, where I am enduring intolerable pains." I saw that bed, writes the saint, and it still makes me shudder; it was bristling with sharp and fiery spikes which entered the flesh. The deceased added that she was suffering this torture for her sloth and negligence in observing the rule. "This is not all," she said again; "My heart is torn in my bosom to punish my murmurs against my superiors; my tongue is eaten by worms for my words contrary to charity and my breaches of silence. But all this is a small matter in comparison with another pain which God made me experience; although it did not last long, it was more painful to me than all my sufferings." The saint, having desired to know what this dire pain was, she replied, "God showed me one of my near female relatives who had died in a state of mortal sin sentenced by the Supreme Judge and dashed into Hell. That sight caused me a fright, horror, pain that no tongue could communicate."

Surius, in the Life of St. Lydwina, relates that, in an ecstasy, this servant of God saw an abyss, the wide opening of which was bordered with flowers, and the great depth of which, when the eye pierced it, chilled with terror. There issued from it an indescribable noise, a frightful mixture of yells, blasphemies, tumult, ringing blows. Her Angel Guardian told her that it was the abode of the damned, and he wanted to show her the torment they suffer. "Alas!" she replied, "I could not bear the sight of them. How could I, as the mere noise of these despairing yells caused me an unbearable horror?"

If the damned suffered no other pain in Hell than to remain there always, without motion, without changing place or position, that alone would be an insupportable torment. A wealthy voluptuary, loaded down with crimes and dreading Hell, did not have the courage either to break off with his evil habits or to expiate his sins by penance. He had recourse to St. Lydwina, who at that time was edifying the world by her patience, and begged her to do penance for him. "Willingly," she replied. "I will offer my sufferings for you on condition that for the space of one night you keep the same position in your bed, without changing sides, budging or stirring."

He readily consented. But, having lain down in bed, he had scarcely rested half an hour when he felt uncomfortable and wished to move. Nevertheless, he did not do it and remained immovable, but the discomfort went on increasing, so much so that at the end of an hour it seemed intolerable to him. Then a salutary reflection sprang up in his mind: "If it is such a torture," he said to himself, "to remain without motion upon a comfortable bed for the space of one night, what would it be, if I were bound down on a bed of fire for the space of a century, of an eternity? And do I fear to redeem such a punishment by a little penance?"

St. Christina, a virgin, justly surnamed "The Admirable," born at St. Trond in 1150, after her death came to life again and lived afterward for 42 years, enduring unheard of sufferings for the relief of the souls in Purgatory and the conversion of sinners.

After a youth spent in innocence, patience and humility, Christina died in the odor of sanctity at the age of 32 years (1182). Her body was borne to the Church of Notre Dame, in which her obsequies were to be celebrated, and it was placed in the middle of the nave, after the manner of that period, in an open coffin. The great throng of people, who were present were praying devoutly, when at the time of the Agnus Dei, the deceased lifted herself up in her coffin, and a few seconds after, with the lightness of a bird, shot up toward the dome and sat calmly on a cornice. At this sight the whole congregation took to flight in a panic; the eldest sister of Christina alone stayed in the church with the priest, who finished the Sacrifice. As soon as he came down from the altar, having ascertained what had happened, he commanded Christina to descend. She obeyed instantly, came down softly, as if her body had no weight, and calmly returned home with her sister.

There, being questioned by her friends and relations, she spoke to them thusly: "When I had given my last sigh, my soul, gone out of my body, found itself surrounded by a troop of angels, who bore it to a dark and frightful place in which there was an innumerable multitude of human souls. There I saw pains and torments which no tongue could express. Among those who were enduring them I noticed many whom I had known on earth. At the sight of their cruel sufferings, I was penetrated with the liveliest compassion, and I asked my guides what this place was. I scarcely doubted that it was Hell, but they replied that it was Purgatory."

"Afterward, they showed me the tortures of the damned; there I saw, also, a few unhappy creatures I had once known."

"Then the angels bore me to the heights of Heaven, before the eternal throne of God. The look, full of love, with which the Most High greeted me, filled my soul with an unspeakable joy. I felt that for all eternity I should enjoy His Blessed Presence.

Answering my thoughts, the Lord said to me: 'Yes, My daughter, you will be eternally with Me, but for the moment, I leave you the choice either to enjoy beatitude from now on, or to return again to earth, there to suffer in a mortal body the pains of the immortal souls (in Purgatory), these pains, however, being unable to cause any damage to your body. By these sufferings you will deliver the souls that have inspired you with so lively a pity, and you will contribute powerfully to the conversion and sanctification of the living. When you shall have filled up the time of this mission, you shall return here again, and enter into the possession of My kingdom.'

"Such was the choice of God proposed to me. I did not hesitate; I chose the part of charity; and God, visibly satisfied with my choice, commanded the angels to bring me to earth."

"My friends," added the saint, "be not astonished at the excess of the wonders which you shall see wrought in my person. They will be the work of God, who does what He pleases, and who acts in everything by designs often hidden, but always adorable."

Upon hearing these words, it may well be understood that the hearers were struck with a holy dread; they looked at Christina with astonishment and trembled at the thought of the sufferings which this woman, returned to life, was going to endure. Indeed, from that moment on, quite different from what she had been before her death, Christina seemed to be a soul from Purgatory in a mortal body. Her life was nothing more than a tissue of unheard-of marvels ad sufferings.

She abandoned human society and lived habitually in solitude. After having assisted in the morning at Mass--at which she often approached the Holy Table -- she was observed fleeing to the woods and wild places, there to spend days and nights in prayer. Endowed with the gift of agility, she flew from one place to another with the speed of lightning, darted to the tops of trees, the roofs of houses, the towers of churches and castles. Often passersby would see her resting on the branches of a tree, then taking flight and disappearing at their approach.

Using no shelter, she lived like the birds of the woods, exposed to all the hardships of the weather, even in the most severe season. Her dress was modest, but excessively coarse and poor. She ate, like animals, what she found in the streets. If she saw a fire lighted, she would plunge her hands or feet into it, or if she could, her whole body altogether, and would endure as long as possible this torture. She used to watch for the opportunity of entering glowing furnaces, red-hot limekilns, and sink as deeply as she could into hot boilers. In winter, she spent the night in the icy water of the rivers; at times she would allow herself to be borne by the current upon mill-wheels, cling to them, suffering herself to be dragged by the machine which struck and broke her against obstacles. Another ingenuity of her passion for torments was to tease packs of dogs so as to be bitten and torn by these animals. At times she rolled in the bushes and thorns until she was covered with blood.

These are some of the means by which she tortured her body; and wonderful circumstance, but conformable to the promise which God had made to her, as soon as she emerged from her torture, she retained no wound of it; her body was untouched and without the least lesion. This life of sufferings served for the edification of a countless multitude of the faithful who were witnesses of it for the space of 42 years, during which the saint still lived. She also converted a great number of sinners, and finally went to enjoy the glory of the elect in the year 1224.

If such mortification makes us shudder, what are we to think of the tortures of the other life? "There," says the author of the Imitation, "one hour in torment will be more terrible than a hundred years spent here below in the most rigorous penance." (Book 1, Chap. 24).

The history of Japan speaks of the horrible abysses of Mount Ungen, situated not far from Nagasaki. Its lofty summit is divided into three craters, the intervals between which form frightful pits; forth from these shoot momentarily into the air eddies of flames, corroding waters and burning mud, which carry such stinking exhalations with them that these abysses pass in the country for the sewers of Hell. All the animals shun them with horror, and the very birds do not fly with impunity over them, however high they soar. The tyrant, Bungondono, the Prince of Ximbara, resolved to dash the Christians headforemost into these frightful chasms. Let the frightful agony they must suffer there be imagined! It was an agony to which death was not to come and put an end, for the consolation of dying was not left to them. Before they were suffocated, they were carefully drawn out to let them regain their breath. Then, soaked as they were by the sulphurous waters, the bodies of the martyrs were covered with frightful pus sacs and were soon but one wound; all their flesh dropped into putrefaction. In this condition they were abandoned like corpses, cast into the common sewer. Are these torments the torments of Hell? They are only a shadow of them.

he same Bungondono devised unheard of tortures to combat Christianity in Japan. One day seven Christians were led before him; they displayed great joy to suffer for the name of Jesus Christ. At this sight, inflamed with rage, the tyrant caused seven ditches to be dug, in which seven crosses were erected; he had the martyrs bound to them and ordered their limbs to be sawed with sharp-edged canes and at the same time salt thrown into their wounds. This torture was executed with a cruel slowness; it lasted five whole days. By an abominable use of the art destined for the preservation of men, the physicians had cordials taken to the martyrs to prolong their sufferings. Is this one of the tortures of Hell? It is only a shadow of them.

At the time of the inroads of the Calvinists into Holland in the 16th century, those sectaries, having seized at Maestricht some priests of the Company of Jesus, resolved to practice all the cruelty of their fanatical hatred upon them. After having overwhelmed them with contempt and outrages, they put round their necks iron collars provided with knives and sharp spikes, they encircled their arms and legs with similar rings, then seated them on seats bristling with nails, so that the martyrs could neither rest nor move without pain. They surrounded them with flames, to burn them slowly. What torture! If the sufferers remained motionless, they were burned; if they moved, they were torn by the spikes and knives. The servants of God triumphed by the help of grace over all this barbarity; it is true, nevertheless, that their torments were atrocious. Now, are these the torments of Hell? They are but the shadow of them.

Antiquity has preserved the names of three tyrants: Mezentius, Actiolinus and Phalaris. The first, Mezentius, it is said, chained his victims to corpses and left them in that revolting state until the infection and putrid inhalations of the dead killed the living. Actiolinus had such frightful dungeons that the condemned used to ask as a favour to be strangled, not to enter them. This grace would be denied; they were lowered with ropes into these stinking caves, there to be buried alive in putrefaction. Phalaris used to shut up his victims in a brazen bull, which he then surrounded with flames to burn them in this manner, while alive. All these pains are horrible, but they are only a shadow of the pains of Hell.

The Romans punished parricides (i.e., those who murdered their parents) by a special kind of torture. The guilty person was tied up in a sack with serpents, and thus cast into the depth of the sea; a feeble image of the torture reserved for those who are guilty of parricide toward God. We shudder when reading in history the description of the frightful torments which the assassin of William, Prince of Orange, had to endure. His body was lacerated by iron rods. Sharp spikes were driven into his flesh; then he was exposed to the action of a slow fire, which caused him inexpressible pains, and, just as he was on the point of expiring, after his hands had been burned with a red iron, he was torn asunder by horses.

That unhappy man committed an enormous crime, but he attacked only a mortal prince. What will not be the chastisement of one who has assailed the King of Kings?

According to certain historians, the Emperor Zeno, a prince as impious as he was dissolute, died by a most tragic death. On the night of April 9, 491, after an excess at table, he fell into so violent a coma that he was believed to be dead, and he was hurriedly buried in the imperial burial vault. There, having regained consciousness, he called in vain for his servants and his guards; no one answered his shouts; he beheld himself in darkness, shut up with the dead on all sides, meeting only cold walls and iron doors. Then giving way to all the transports of rage and despair, he dashed himself against his surroundings and broke his skull against the walls. It was in this terrible state that his corpse was discovered. What a horrible situation for that prince, buried alive! Is that the situation of the reprobate?

Hell is the sink of the world and the receptacle of all the moral filth of humanity. There, impurity, intemperance, blasphemy, pride, injustice and all the vices which are like the rottenness of souls, are found heaped up. To this moral filth a corporal stench is added more insupportable than all the stenches of hospitals and corpses. If the body of a damned person, says St. Bonaventure, were deposited on the earth, that of itself alone would be sufficient to make the earth uninhabitable; it would fill it with its infection, as a corpse that might be left to rot in a house would infect it all the way through.

A man at Lyons had gone into a burial vault in which a corpse lately buried was found wholly putrefied. Scarcely had he gone down when he fell dead. The poisonous exhalations caught him so violently that he was suffocated.

Sulpicius Severus narrates in the life of St. Martin of Tours, that towards the end of the saint's life the demon came to tempt him under a visible form. The spirit of lies appeared before him with royal magnificence, a crown of gold on his head, and said he was the King of Glory, Christ, the Son of God. The holy bishop recognized the tempter under these appearances of human grandeur and chased him away with contempt. Proud Satan was confounded; he disappeared, but for his revenge, he left the holy man's room filled with a stench that did not allow him to remain there any more.

Another torture of hell is the horrible society of the devils and the damned. There are some wretched sinners who, seeing plainly that they are walking toward Hell, are comforted by saying, "I shall not be there alone!" Sad consolation! It is that of the convicts sentenced to wear irons together in the galleys. Still it is intelligible how a convict finds a certain life in the company of his kind. Alas! It will not be thus in Hell, in which the damned will be mutual executioners. "There," says St. Thomas, "the associates of his wretchedness, far from alleviating the lot of the damned soul, will make it more intolerable for him." (Suppl. 9, 86, A. 1). The society of even those persons who on earth were their best friends is insupportable to the damned in Hell. They would esteem themselves happy to have tigers and lions for companions, rather than their relatives, brothers, or their own parents.

Do you wish to see the poverty of hell and the privations that are suffered there by those who made the goods of this world their god? Consider the wicked rich man of the Gospel. Accustomed during his life to eat delicate meats served in silver utensils, to drink exquisite wines in goblets of gold, to wear purple and fine linen, having become an inhabitant of Hell, he found himself brought down to the last extremity of need. He who refused poor Lazarus the crumbs from his table, was obliged to beg in his turn. He asks, not delicacies, but a drop of cold water, which he will be happy to receive from a leper's finger. Now, this drop of water is refused to him. Has not the Savior said: "Woe to you that are rich, for you have your consolation. Woe to you that are filled, for you shall hunger." (Luke 6:25).

"There is no light," writes St. Teresa (Autobiography, Chapter 25), "in the eternal pit, only darkness of the deepest dye; and yet, O mystery! Although no light shines, all that can be most painful to the sight is perceived. Among those objects which torture the eyes of the damned, the most frightful are the demons, who reveal themselves in all their hideousness. St. Bernard speaks of a religious who, being in his cell, uttered all of a sudden frightful cries, which attracted the community. He was found beside himself and uttering only these sorrowful words: "Accursed be the day I entered religion!" Terrified and troubled by this curse, the cause of which they did not understand, his brethren questioned and encouraged him and spoke to him of confidence in God. Soon, being quieted, he replied, "no, no, it is not the religious life that I should curse. On the contrary, blessed be the day I became a religious! My brethren, do not be astonished at seeing my mind disturbed. Two devils have appeared to me; their horrible appearance has put me out of my senses. What monstrosity! Ah! Rather all torments than again to endure the sight of them!"

A holy priest was exorcising a demoniac, and he asked the demon what pains he was suffering in Hell. "An eternal fire," he answered, "an eternal malediction, an eternal rage, and a frightful despair at being never able to gaze upon Him who created me." "What would you do to have the happiness of seeing God?" "To see Him but for one moment, I should willingly consent to endure my torments for 10,000 years. But vain desires! I shall suffer forever and never see Him!"

On a like occasion, the exorcist inquired of the demon what was his greatest pain in Hell. He replied with an accent of indescribable despair: "Always, always! Never, never!"

One day, a holy soul was meditating upon Hell, and considering the eternity of the pains, the frightful "always... never," she was thrown into complete confusion by it, because she was unable to reconcile this immeasurable severity with the divine goodness and other perfections. "Lord," she said, "I submit to Thy judgments, but do not push the rigors of Thy justice to far." "Do you understand," was the answer, "what sin is? To sin is to say to God, I will not serve Thee! I despise Thy law, I laugh at Thy threats!" "I understand, Lord, that sin is an outrage to Thy Majesty." "Well, measure, if you can, the greatness of this outrage." "Lord, this outrage is infinite, since it attacks infinite Majesty." "Must it not, then, be punished by an infinite chastisement? Now, as the punishment could not be infinite in its intensity, justice demands that it be so at least in its duration. Accordingly, it is the divine justice that wills the eternity of the pains: the terrible 'always,' the terrible 'never.' The damned themselves will be obliged to render homage to this justice, and cry out in the midst of their torments: "Thou art just, O Lord, and thy judgments are equitable.'" (Psalm 118: 137).

St. John Damascene relates, in the life of St. Josaphat, that this young prince, being one day exposed to violent temptations, prayed to God with tears to be delivered from them. His prayer was graciously heard; he was caught up in an ecstasy, and he beheld himself led to a dark place, full of horror, confusion, and frightful spectres. There was a pool of sulphur and fire in which were plunged innumerable wretches, a prey to devouring flames. Amid the despairing howls and shouts, he heard a heavenly voice, which uttered these words: "Here it is that sin receives its punishment; here it is that a moment's pleasure is punished by an eternity of torments." This vision filled him with new strength, and enabled him to triumph over all the assaults of the enemy.

The most bitter regret of the damned will be, says St. Thomas, to be damned for "nothing," while they might have so easily obtained everlasting happiness.

Jonathan was condemned to death for having eaten a little honey, against the prohibition of Saul. In his misfortune he said, while moaning, "Alas! I did but taste a little honey.. and behold I must die!" (1 Samuel 14:43).

More bitter will be the regrets of the damned when they shall see that, for a "honeycomb," for a fleeting enjoyment, they have incurred everlasting death.

King Lysimachus, besieged by the Scythians, who had cut off all the springs, beheld himself reduced to the last extremity by lack of water. Yielding to the craving of his thirst, he surrendered to the enemy, who left him only his life safe. Then a cup of water was given him to quench his thirst. When he had drunk it, he said, "Oh, how quickly has the pleasure passed for which I have lost my throne and my liberty!" It is in this manner that the damned will speak, but with far more bitterness: Oh, how quickly passed the guilty pleasure for which I forfeited an eternal crown and happiness!

Esau returned faint from the chase, and seeing Jacob, who was cooking lentils, he sold him his birthright for a dish of the pottage. "And so taking bread and the pottage of lentils," says the Scripture, "he ate and drank, and then went his way, making little account of having sold his birthright." But when the time came to receive his inheritance when he saw the large portion given to his brother and the small portion that was left to him, "He was filled with consternation, and uttered a great cry." Then, having sought in vain to better his lot, he yielded to the bitterest regrets and filled the air with his doleful cries; they were less cries than roars. "Irriguit clamore magno." ("He roared out, with a great cry." (Gen. 25, 27:34). What will be the cries of the damned when they shall see that they have sold their heavenly inheritance for less than "a dish of pottage"--when they shall see that for a trifle they have sold everlasting benefits and incurred everlasting torments?

The prophet Jeremias had warned Sedecias King of Juda, of the future that awaited him, he had spoken to him on behalf of God. "Behold life, and behold death; if you observe my words, you shall remain quiet on your throne; if you trample them under foot, I will deliver you into the hands of the King of Babylon." (Jerem. 29:39). Sedecias paid no attention to these warnings of God, and soon the chastisements foretold fell upon him; he was delivered to Nebuchadnezzar, blinded, loaded with chains, and thrown into the prison of Babylon. Then, what were not his regrets, his grief, at the remembrance of the words of Jeremias? A weak image of the tardy regrets, the cruel sorrows that devour the damned.

They weep for the time they lost in vain amusements and in forgetfulness of their salvation. "One hour," they say, "would have given us what an eternity could give us back no more!" Father Nieremberg relates that a servant of God, finding himself in a secluded place into which no other man had ventured, heard mournful wails, which could proceed only from a supernatural cause. He demanded, then, who were the authors of these piteous cries and what they meant. Then a sad voice replied to him: "We are the damned. Let it be known that we are deploring in Hell the time lost, the precious time which we waste on earth in vanities and crime. Ah! One hour would have given us what an eternity could restore to us no more."

VIII. A SALUTARY FEAR OF HELL

We ought to believe in Hell, because we may fall into it. Alas! It is very easy to be damned, and the damned are very numerous. St. Teresa compares them to the flakes of snow which fall in the dreary days of winter. The servant of God, Anthony Pereyra, in a very authentic vision with which he was favoured (see Ch. 2), saw the souls of sinners descending into the pit like corn beneath the millstones, like stones cast in heaps into a huge limekiln. God showed one day before a large multitude that they fall into it as the dead leaves in autumn fall from the trees under the breath of the wind.

The venerable Father Anthony Baldinucci, a celebrated missionary of the Company of Jesus, who died in the odor of sanctity in the year 1717, was preaching in the open air, because the church could not contain the faithful who came in crowds to hear him. Speaking of Hell, he said, "My brethren, would you know how great is the number of those who are damned? Look at that tree." All eyes were turned to a tree that was there, covered with leaves. At the same moment a gust of wind, rising, shook all the branches of the tree, and caused the leaves to fall so plentifully that there remained only a certain number of them, thinly scattered and easy to count. "See," went on the man of God, "what souls are lost, and what souls are saved. Take your precautions to be among the latter."

Father Nieremberg speaks of a bishop, who by a special permission of God, received a visit from an unhappy sinner who had died impenitent a short time before. Addressing the prelate, this damned soul demanded if there were men still on earth. As the bishop seemed astonished at this question, the lost soul added: "Since I have been in that melancholy abode, I have seen such a prodigious multitude arrive, that I am at a loss to conceive that there are men still on earth." This speech recalls that of the Savior in the Gospel. "Enter ye in at the narrow gate; for wide is the gate, and broad is the way that leadeth to destruction, and many there are who go in thereat. How narrow is the gate and strait is the way that leadeth to life; and few there are that find it!" (Matt. 7:13-14).

To avoid Hell, it is necessary to avoid the road to it, and to destroy the cause of damnation, that is, sin, under all its forms. Men permit themselves to be allured to their ruin by different bonds of iniquity, sometimes by one, sometimes by another. There are many who die in their sins because they are deprived of the Last Sacraments, and among those who receive them, there are not a few who are lost because they lack sincerity in the accusation of their sins. Here is an incident which we read in the Annals of Paraguay, during the year 1640. In the Reduction (Jesuit mission plantation) of the Assumption, a woman died who had left a son of about 20 years. This young man beheld his mother appear to him in the most frightful condition. She told him that she was damned for not having made a sincere Confession, and that many others were damned like her for having concealed their sins in Confession. "And you," she added, "do profit by the example of your unfortunate mother."

Father Nieremberg mentions also another damned person who revealed the cause of his damnation. A young man was leading an apparently Christian life, but he had an enemy whom he hated, and while frequenting the Sacraments, he all the while harboured in his heart sentiments of ill-will and revenge, which Jesus Christ commands to be discarded. After his death, he appeared to his father and told him that he was damned for not having forgiven his enemy, after which he exclaimed with an accent of unutterable sorrow: "Ah! If all the stars in Heaven were so many tongues of fire, they could not express what torments I endure!"

Let us listen again to the same author. An unhappy man who had the habit of taking pleasure in immodest thoughts fell sick and received the Last Sacraments. The next day his confessor, going to visit him again, saw him on the road coming to meet him. "Go no further," he said to him, "I am dead and damned." "How?" demanded the priest. "Did you not make a good confession of your sins?" "Yes, I made a good confession, but afterwards the devil represented to me sinful pleasures, and asked me whether in case of a cure I should not return again to my pleasures? I consented to these evil suggestions, and at the same moment death surprised me." Then, opening his garment, he showed the fire that was devouring him and disappeared.

We read also in Father Nieremberg that a noble lady, who was exceedingly pious, asked God to make known to her what displeased His Divine Majesty most in persons of her sex. The Lord vouchsafed in a miraculous manner to hear her. He opened under her eyes the Eternal Abyss. There she saw a woman a prey to cruel torments and in her recognized one of her friends, a short time before deceased. This sight caused her as much astonishment as grief: the person whom she saw damned did not seem to her to have lived badly.

Then that unhappy soul said to her: "It is true that I practiced religion, but I was a slave of vanity. Ruled by the passion to please, I was not afraid to adopt indecent fashions to attract attention, and I kindled the fire of impurity in more than one heart. Ah! If Christian women knew how much immodesty in dress displeases God!" At the same moment, this unhappy soul was pierced by two fiery lances, and plunged into a caldron of liquid lead.

Thomas of Cantimpre, a learned religious of the Order of St. Dominic, relates that there was at Brussels an unhappy sinner, the slave of intemperance and the other vices which it foments. He had a friend, the companion of his dissipation, to whom he was greatly attached. A sudden death put an end to his disorders. His sorrowful companion, after having accompanied him to the grave, had returned home and was alone in his chamber, when he heard moans underground. Frightened at first and not knowing what to do, he ventured at length to ask who it was that he heard moaning. "It is I, your companion, whose body you attended to the grave. Alas! My soul is buried in Hell." Then, uttering a cry, or rather a dreadful roar, he added, "Woe to me! The abyss has swallowed me, and the pit has closed its mouth upon me."

Louis of Granada speaks of a young woman whose damnation had no other source than vanity and the desire to please. She led a regular life, but her passion to attract attention by the charm of her beauty was the moving cause of her whole conduct. Having fallen sick, she died, having received all the Sacraments. While her confessor was praying for her soul, she appeared to him, saying that she was damned, and that the cause of her damnation was vanity. "I sought," she added, "only to please the eyes of men. This passion caused me to commit a multitude of sins; it prevented me from receiving the Sacraments well, and it has led me to everlasting torments."

A usurer had two sons who followed the evil example of their father. One of the two, touched by God, forsook his guilty profession and retired to the desert. Before setting out, he exhorted his father and brother with tears to think, like him, of the salvation of their souls. It was to no purpose; they persevered in sin, and died in a state of impenitence. God permitted the solitary to know their unhappy condition. In an ecstasy he saw himself on a high mountain at the foot of which was a sea of fire, from which arose confused cries, like a tempest. Soon, in the midst of these burning waves, he perceived his father and brother, furiously raging against each other, mutually upbraiding and cursing each other and holding this dreadful dialogue: "I curse thee, detestable son! It is for thee that I did injustice and lost my soul." "I curse thee, unworthy father, who ruined me by thy bad example." "I curse thee, foolish son, who joined thy father in his sins." "I curse thee, the author of my life, who reared me up for damnation!" Behold how wicked parents and wicked children will eternally rend one another by reciprocal maledictions. (Lives of the Fathers of the Desert).

IX. THE THOUGHT OF HELL

St. Dositheus, who lived in the eleventh century, was brought up as a page at the Court of Constantinople, and at first led a life altogether worldly, in a profound ignorance of the truths of faith. As he had heard a great deal about Jerusalem, he visited it out of a motive of curiosity. There it was that God's mercy was awaiting him. To touch him, it made use of a picture placed in a church representing the pains of Hell. Miserable souls were seen there in despair, plunged in a sea of fire, in which horrible monsters were tormenting them and making game of the tortures. Struck by these terrible scenes, Dositheus demanded the explanation of them from an unknown person who was there. "It is Hell," answered this person; "they are the pains of the damned." "How long will these pains last? Why are they damned? Might I myself fall into such a terrible state of woe? What must I do to be safe from Hell?" Such were the questions that Dositheus by turns proposed to the person who was instructing him. He was impressed by the answers to such a degree that he quit the world that very hour to go and live in seclusion. He entered a monastery in which, thanks to the thought of Hell, which he had always before his eyes, and to the wise direction of the Abbot whom he found there, he made rapid progress in the ways of God.

Whoever thinks of Hell will not fall into it, because in the time of temptation this thought will retain him in his duty. St. Martinian had lived 25 years in solitude when God allowed his fidelity to be put to a violent test. A perfidious woman, the courtesan Zoe, came to solicit him to sin. She was disguised as a mendicant, and taking advantage of a rain storm, knocked at the cell of Martinian, begging shelter from him. The holy anchorite could not refuse it in these circumstances. He let the stranger in and having lighted a fire, invited her to dry her garments. But soon the unfortunate woman, casting off the borrowed rags she wore, appeared to the eyes of Martinian in a most brilliant dress and with all her fascinating charms. The servant of God, in the presence of a most dreadful danger, remembered Hell, and drawing near the fire, which was blazing on the hearth, he took off his shoes and plunged both feet into the fire. The pain drew cries from him, but he said to his soul, "Alas! My soul, if thou canst not bear so weak a fire, how wilt thou be able to bear the fire of Hell?" The temptation was overcome, and Zoe was converted. Such was the salutary effect of the thought of hell.

Another recluse, assailed by a violent temptation and afraid of being conquered, lighted his lamp. Then, to be penetrated vividly with the thought of Hell, he put his fingers into the flame and let them burn there with inexpressible sufferings. "Since thou dost wish," he said, addressing himself, "to sin and accept Hell, which will be the punishment of thy sin, try first if thou shalt have the courage to support the pain of an everlasting fire."

It is related that St. Philip Neri received one day a visit from a man who was leading a sinful life. Imbued with the most unfriendly feelings toward the saint, this visitor addressed him with the most unjust reproaches and heaped insults upon him. His anger was such that he was incapable of listening to reason. Then St. Philip made him draw near the chimney, and pointing out the place where the fire was made, he said, "Look at this fireplace." The sinner looked, but instead of a fireplace, he saw a pit all on fire, in the bottom of which he recognized a place that was destined for him. Seized with fright, this furious sinner grew calm, suddenly recognized the evil state of his soul, and changed his life.

In 1815 the young Louis Francis de Beauvais died at the College of St. Acheul near Amiens. He was only 14 years old, but he was ripe for Heaven, so innocent and holy had been his life. Such solid virtue in so tender a youth was due to the thought of Hell. One day, while still quite a child, he was seated at his mother's side before a warm fire. "Mamma," he asked her, "could the fire of Hell be as hot as this?" "Alas, my child, this fire is nothing in comparison to Hell!" "Well, if I should fall into it?" he rejoined with fright. "Hell," said his mother, "is only for sinners. If you keep away from sin, you have nothing to fear." This idea was engraved in the heart of Louis Francis; it was the source of his sorrow of sin and of his holy life.

In 1540 Blessed Peter Lefevre, one of the first companions of St. Ignatius of Loyola, returning from Parma to Rome, while following the way from Florence to Siena, was overcome by nightfall in the midst of a country infested by robbers and brigands. He had recourse, as was his wont, to his Angel Guardian, and perceived pretty soon a house, at which he asked hospitality. It was in the month of October; the weather was cold and rainy. The people who dwelt at the manor, seeing that the traveller was a priest, welcomed him with respect and kindness, offered him refreshments, and invited him to draw near the fire to dry his clothes. While he was seated near the hearth and speaking with his hosts of the things of God, a noise of hurried steps was heard, then violet rapping at the door, and behold, men armed to the teeth dashed into the house. It was a band of brigands. They were 16 and demanded noisily that all the provisions in store should be given to them; then, having ranged themselves round a table, they set to drinking and eating amid rude songs and immodest conversation.

Blessed Peter Lefevre was not taken aback; he remained seated, calm, pensive, his eyes fixed on the fire. The leader of the bandits asked him what he was doing there. The man of God did not reply at first. "You do not answer," remarked the brigand. "Are you deaf? Are you dumb?" "No," he replied then, "but a thought occupies my mind." "What is this great thought? Tell us. What are you thinking of?" "I am thinking," he said, in a calm, grave tone, "that the joy of sinners is very sad; this fire brings to my mind that of Hell, which they shall not be able to escape, if they do not hasten to return sincerely to God." These words were spoken with a force and unction that struck these savage men with respect. They said not a word more, and the servant of God took advantage of their attention to speak to them of the danger that they ran of falling into the hands of human justice, and still more, into those of God's justice; then he touched on the security of a good conscience and the mercy of

God, of whom he spoke in language so touching that he caused them to melt into tears, and demand forgiveness of their sins. He encouraged them and prepared them so well, that the whole 16 made their confessions to him that night.

The thought of Hell fortifies the weakest. Two early Christians, Domnina and Theomilla, were brought before the Roman Prefect Lysias, who gave them notice of the order to renounce the Faith in order to adore idols. They absolutely refused. Then Lysias had a funeral pyre lighted, and the altar of the false gods set up. "Choose," he said to them, "either to burn incense on the altar of our gods or to be yourselves burned in the flames of this pyre." They replied, without hesitating a moment: "We fear not this burning pile, which will be soon extinguished; the fire we do fear is that of Hell, which never goes out. Not to fall into it, we detest your idols and we adore Jesus Christ." They underwent martyrdom in the year 235.

Caesarius relates that a wicked man, for whom many prayers had been offered, fell sick and died. As he was going to be buried, he came back to life again, and rose up full of strength, but seized with an exceeding alarm. Interrogated concerning what had happened to him, he answered, "God has just granted me a signal favour; He showed me Hell, an immense ocean of fire, into which I was about to be plunged for my sins. A delay was accorded to me, that I might redeem my sins by penance." Thenceforth, this sinner was changed into a different man. He thought no more of anything save of expiating his sins by his tears, fasts and prayers. He used to walk barefooted on brambles and thorns; he lived on bread and water only, and gave to the poor whatever he earned by his labour. When people would prevail upon him to moderate his austerities, he would reply, "I have seen Hell; I know that too much cannot be done to avoid it. Ah, Hell! If all the trees and all the forests were heaped up in a vast pile and set on fire, I should prefer to remain in that burning fire to the end of the world, rather than endure for only one hour the fire of Hell."

The Venerable Bede speaks of a rich inhabitant of Northumberland, whom the sight of Hell changed after a like fashion into a new man. He was called Trithelmus, and he led a worldly life, pretty much like that of the wicked rich man of the Gospel. God, by an exceptional mercy, granted him a vision, in which He showed him the eternal pains of the damned. Having come back to himself again, Trithelmus confessed all his sins, distributed all his wealth to the poor, and went into a monastery, where he put no bounds to his austerities and penances. In winter he stood in the freezing water; in summer he endured the burden of heat and toil; he practiced vigorous fasts and continued his mortifications to the last stage of his life. When he was spoken to about diminishing his penances, he would reply, "If you had seen, like me, the pains of Hell, you would talk otherwise." "But how can you keep up such severe mortifications?" "I count them as nothing beside the pains of Hell, which I have deserved by my sins."

Mgr. de Segur narrates a rather singular fact which happened at the Military School of St. Cyr in the last years of the Restoration. The Abbe Rigolot, the almoner of the institution, was preaching a retreat to the pupils who assembled every evening in the chapel before retiring to the dormitory.

A certain evening when the worthy almoner had spoken on Hell, the exercises being finished, he was retiring, with a small candlestick in his hand, to his room, which was situated in a wing reserved for the officers. Just as he opened his door, he heard himself called by someone who was following him up the staircase. It was an old captain with a gray moustache and by no means elegant appearance.

"Pardon, Monsieur Almoner," he said in a slightly ironical tone of voice, "you have just given us a very fine sermon on Hell; only you forgot to tell us whether, in the fire of Hell, we should be grilled or roasted or boiled. Could you tell me?" The almoner seeing whom he had to deal with, looked at him straight in the eye and putting the candlestick under his nose, quietly replied, "You shall see this, Captain!" and he shut his door, unable to refrain from laughing somewhat at the silly, baffled expression on the face of the poor captain.

He thought of it no more, but from that time forth he fancied that the captain used to take to his heels from him, as far as possible. The Revolution of July came on. The military almonery was abolished, that of St. Cyr like the rest. The Abbe Rigolot was nominated by the Archbishop of Paris to another position not less honourable.

Twenty years after, the venerable priest was one evening in a drawing room, in which there was a numerous gathering, when he saw coming toward him an old man with a white moustache, who asked him if he were not the Abbe Rigolot, at one time almoner of St. Cyr. And upon his affirmative reply, the old soldier said with emotion, "O Monsieur Almoner, permit me to clasp your hand and express all my gratitude to you: you saved me." "I? And how so?" "Well! You do not know me! Do you remember one evening when a captain, an instructor of the school, having proposed to you, after the close of a sermon on Hell, an exceedingly ridiculous question, you answered him while putting your candlestick under his nose, 'You will see this, Captain?' I am that captain. Fancy, that from that time, your speech pursued me everywhere, as well as the thought that I might be burned in Hell. I struggled for ten years, but at last I was forced to surrender: I have been to my confession; I have become a Christian, a Christian in the military fashion, that is to say, like a soldier. It is to you I owe this happiness, and I am very glad to meet you, to be able to tell you so."

Father de Bussy, of the Company of Jesus, gave at the beginning of this century, in a certain large city of the South of France, an important mission, which roused the whole population. It was in the heart of winter; Christmas Day was at hand, and it was very cold. In the room in which the Father was receiving the men, there was a stove with a good fire.

One day the Father saw a young man coming to him who had been recommended to him on account of his dissipation and open parade of impiety. Father de Bussy soon saw there was nothing to be done with him. "Come here, my good friend," he said pleasantly; "I do not hear the confessions of people in spite of themselves. Stay; sit down there, and let us have a little chat while warming ourselves." He opened the stove, and noticed that the wood was going soon to be burned up.

"Before sitting down, pray bring me one or two logs," he said to the young man. The latter, somewhat astonished, did, nevertheless, what the Father asked. "Now," the latter added, "put it in the stove for me; there, very far down in the bottom." And, as the other was getting the wood into the door of the stove, Father de Bussy, all at once, took his arm, and plunged it into the bottom of the stove.

The young man uttered a shout and sprang backward. "Ah me!" he shouted. "Are you crazy? You were going to burn me?" "What ails you, my dear man?" remarked the father calmly; "should you not get accustomed to it? In Hell, where you shall go if you continue your present course of life, it will not be merely the tips of the fingers that shall be burned by the fire, but your whole body, and this little fire is nothing to the other one. Come, come, my good friend, be brave; you must get accustomed to everything burning." The young libertine went away in a thoughtful mood. He was reflecting indeed; he did reflect so well that he was not slow in coming back again to the missionary, who helped him to get rid of his faults and enter anew on the good path.

I affirm, adds Mgr. de Segur, that of a thousand, ten thousand men who live far from God, and therefore on the way to Hell, there would not be one, perhaps, who could resist the test of fire. There would not be one who should be so crazy as to accept this bargain: During the year, you may yield to all your passions, gratify all your whims, on the condition of spending one day, only one day, or even one hour, in fire. I repeat, not a single person would accept the bargain. Will you have a proof of it? Listen to the history of the three sons of an old usurer.

A father of a family who grew rich only by doing wrongs had fallen dangerously ill. He knew that the final stages of death had already set in, and nevertheless he could not decide to make restitution. "If I make restitution," he said, "what will become of my children?"

His confessor, a man of sagacity, had recourse to a singular stratagem to save this poor soul. He told him that if he wished to be cured, he was about to give him an extremely simple, but costly remedy. "Should it cost a thousand, two thousand, even ten thousand francs, what odds?" answered the old man briskly. "What is it?" "It consists in pouring the melted fat of a living person on the dying parts. It does not need much. If you find anyone willing, for ten thousand francs, to suffer one hand to be burned for less than a quarter of an hour, that will be enough."

"Alas!" said the poor man, sighing, "I am very much afraid I can find no such person." "I will help you," said the priest quietly. "Summon your eldest son; he loves you; he is to be your heir; say to him, 'My dear son, you can save your old father's life, if you consent to allow one hand to be burned only for a small quarter of an hour.' If he refuses, make the proposal to the second, pledging yourself to make him your heir at the expense of his eldest brother. If he refuses in his turn, the third will no doubt accept."

The proposition was made successively to the three brothers, who, one after the other, rejected it with a shudder. Then the father said to them: "What! To save my life, an instant's pain alarms you? And I, to procure your comfort, would go to Hell--to be burned eternally! Indeed, I should be quite mad." And he hastened to restore all he owed without regard to what should become of his children. He was quite right, and so were his three sons. To suffer a hand to be burned, a short quarter of an hour, even to save a father's life, is a sacrifice above human strength.

In 1844, again writes Mgr. de Segur, I was acquainted at the Seminary of St. Sulpice at Issy, near Paris, with an extremely distinguished professor of science, and a man whose humility and mortification were admired by everyone. Before becoming a priest, the Abbe Pinault had been one of the most eminent professors of the Polytechnic School. In the seminary he taught the course of physics and chemistry. One day, during an experiment, the fire somehow caught the phosphorus he was manipulating, and in a moment his hand was wrapped in flames. Assisted by his pupils, the poor professor tried to no purpose to put out the fire that was eating into his flesh. In a few minutes his hand was but a shapeless, shining mass; the nails had disappeared. Overcome by the excess of pain, the unfortunate professor lost consciousness. His hand and arm were plunged into a pail of cold water to try to assuage a little of the violence of this martyrdom. All day and all night he uttered but one cry, an irresistible and heartrending cry; and when, now and then, he could utter a few words, he would say and say again to the three or four seminarians who were waiting on him: "O my children! My children! Do not go to Hell! Do not go to Hell!"

A brother, named John Baptist, was living at the time of St. Ignatius at the profession-house in Rome. He was remarkable for the spirit of fervor and mortification which he derived from the thought of Hell. As he filled the humble office of cook the fire, which he had incessantly under his eyes, reminded him of the fire of divine justice, which shall torment eternally the impious in Hell, and caused him to conceive a great horror for sin, which merits such horrible chastisements. One day, when profoundly absorbed by these thoughts, he yielded to the grief which the sins caused him; he was seized by an attack of indiscreet fervor; he plunged his hand into the fire and there left it burning. The odor which arose from it was smelled by the Father who exercised the office of minister of the house. He came into the kitchen and asked what was the matter. The brother could not conceal the excess of his pain, acknowledged his fault, and falling at his knees, humbly begged his pardon. St. Ignatius was informed of the matter; he was told that this brother had just deprived himself of the use of his hand and had become incapable of doing his work. The Saint considered his fault more worthy of compassion than punishment. He set to prayer and spent a part of the night in it, as was his custom. The next morning the brother's hand was cured and as sound as if it had not been injured. God manifested by this miracle that, if this fervent religious had done an inconsiderate act, the motive that prompted him to do it--that is, the fear of Hell--was agreeable to Him.

St. Teresa had seen the place that was prepared for her in Hell, and the remembrance gave her strength to bear the severest trials. This is how she speaks, in the 32nd chapter of her autobiography: "Being one day in prayer, in an instant I found myself, without knowing how, carried body and soul into Hell. I understood that God wished to make me see the place I should have occupied, had I not changed my life. No words can give the least idea of such suffering--it is beyond comprehension. I felt in my soul a devouring fire, and my body was, at the same time, a prey to intolerable pains. I had endured cruel sufferings during my lifetime, but all that I had suffered was nothing when compared to what I experienced then. What filled up the measure was the prospect that they should be unending and unalleviated. The tortures of the body, however cruel they might have been, were nothing in their turn beside the anguish of the soul. While I felt myself burned, and as if hacked into a thousand pieces, I was suffering all the agonies of death, all the horrors of despair. There was not a particle of hope, of consolation, in this frightful sojourn. There was a pestiferous odor, by which one was continually suffocated. There was no light, only darkness of the sombrest hue; and yet, O prodigy! Though there was no light shining, whatever is most distressing to the sight is seen. In short, all I had heard said of the pains of Hell, all I had read of it in books, was nothing beside the reality. There was the same difference as between a lifeless portrait and a living person. Ah! The hottest fire in this world is such a trifling thing! It is like a painted fire compared to that fire which burns the damned in Hell. Almost ten years have passed since that vision, and I am still seized with such a fright in describing it, that my blood is frozen in my veins. Amid trials and sufferings I call up this remembrance, and it gives me strength to bear all."

The wonderful conversion of an obstinate Protestant lady, which created quite a sensation in

America, was owing to the thought of Hell. This person was none other than the wife of General X., one of the ablest generals of the Northern army in the war of 1860. Here are the particulars of this conversion, as Monsignor Fitzpatrick, Bishop of Boston, related them to St. Michael's College at Brussels, in November, 1862. General X., first a Protestant, had had the happiness of hearing a simple, clear explanation of the Catholic religion. It was sufficient for this upright and noble man to make him see the truth and embrace Catholicism with all his heart. From that time, full of faith and fervor, he devoted himself, not only to living as a true Catholic, but also to procuring for other Protestants the grace of conversion. In a short time he won over 20 officers, and wrote a book destined to furnish instruction for soldiers. We can well understand that he had not forgotten his wife, who was a Protestant, but he had the grief of seeing all the efforts of his zeal fail in this direction. Meanwhile, God permitted Madam X. to be attacked by an illness which reduced her to the last extremity. The General, after having exhausted to no purpose all the resources of faith and charity, seeing the sick woman on the point of dying in her obstinacy, recurred to a last means. He called in four Irishwomen whom he had in his service, and, with tears in his eyes, said to them: "My friends, you know my wife is a Protestant, and that she is unwilling to hear the Catholic religion spoken of. She is going to die in her obstinacy and fall into Hell. I shudder at the thought of such a misfortune; it must be absolutely prevented if it is possible. Let us pray, then, to the holy Virgin and do violence to her merciful heart." Thereupon, the General drew forth his beads, and began to pray on his knees; the poor attendants did the same; the whole five continued pray for one hour. Then the general went to the bed of the invalid and discovered her in a sort of coma, out of her senses, without consciousness. At the end of some time, returning to herself and looking at her husband, she said to him in a very intelligible voice: "Call a Catholic priest." The General believed at first that she was delirious, and made her repeat what she desired. "I beg," she said, "for a Catholic priest without delay." "But my dear, you would not have one." "Ah, General, I am entirely changed. God has shown me Hell, and the place that awaited me in the eternal fire, if I did not become a Catholic." So the sick woman had the happiness of returning to the bosom of the Church. She even recovered her health, and lived afterward as a fervent Catholic. Such was the narrative of the venerable Bishop of

Boston; he had these details from General X's own mouth.

THE END

Hell

Made in United States
North Haven, CT
21 June 2023